Pr

If you want to learn the first steps to buying property today, then this book is for you. The author starts at the beginning and helps those who want to learn what they can do immediately. This easy-to-read investment guide starts by explaining how to save down payments and offers suggestions for the type of loans you can qualify for. It's inspirational to understand that you don't need a trust fund or an inheritance to start an investment career. Super easy and fast read!

Ali Razi | Founder & CEO,
Banc Certified Merchant Services

This book is like a real estate investment course for newbies and proves that anybody can jump in the real estate investment game. I especially loved how the author explained the simplest aspects to buying property. Those folks who are just dipping their toes in the water will be well served to give this book a read and know what to anticipate, where to spend money and where not to spend money. This book will save you a lot of time and mistakes, no doubt!

Mark Nureddine | CEO, Bull Outdoor
Products; best-selling author of *Pocket Mentor*

Anyone who talks to the older generations has heard that it's much harder for our generation to buy properties. Well, if that's true, then you won't let that discourage you after reading this how-to book on investing. The takeaways from this book are that anyone can learn how to invest and you are no exception. Even if you're living paycheck to paycheck, Cripps will show you that you have the power to start from exactly where you are. I'm buying a couple of copies for the people I know who are struggling right now. Thank you, Kristin.

Chris Catranis | CEO, Babylon Telecommunications, best-selling author of *Disruptive Leadership*

Kristin Cripps has written a how-to investment guide for all people from all walks of life. You won't be able to make excuses for why you can't get ahead after reading this easy-to-follow guide to investment. I appreciate that this busy lady is freely sharing her secrets with those wanting to learn exactly where to start. Once you read this book, you'll be able to clearly see the path she followed to build her career from the ground up. I'll be reading this book again and again!

Rick Orford | Co-Founder & Executive Producer at Travel Addicts Life, and best-selling author of *The Financially Independent Millennial*

Love this lady and this book! Kristin tells it like it is and leaves you no excuses for why you can't kick butt in the investment world too. I love reading books that combine humor with learning so this was my perfect type of read. Kristin writes like she's a friend sitting across the table giving you real advice over a cup of coffee. I laughed out loud at her descriptions of the folks who showed up to rent properties: her stories are that real! I'm still laughing, while knowing that anything is possible, including success and weathering crazy situations. I'm glad to hear that she is now a speaker, and I will definitely be attending her speaking engagements in the future.

Tamara Nall | President and CEO at the Leading Niche

Kristin's book was a pleasant surprise. I was hoping it wouldn't be another droll book about investment, and it wasn't. Her stories are real and her snark is hilarious. She learned the ropes on her own, one investment at a time. I particularly appreciated that she shared her occasional failure and now her readers know what to avoid and what not to do. She plays it exactly like it is, and shares the ups and downs of what can go wrong.

Sanjay Jaybhay | Best-selling author of *Invest and Grow Rich*

Kristin Cripps has a gift for teaching while making you laugh at the same time. This book is a perfect gift for anyone thinking about how to start investing in real estate and who wants an enjoyable read. I really liked how she included funny stories about the craziness she faced in the real estate world. I now feel ready to jump in and buy my first property (while avoiding the pitfalls she explained). I feel empowered and educated after reading this book!

Mar Ricketts | Principal & Founder, GuildWorks

This second book by real estate investor Kristin Cripps lays out her easy-to-follow path to success. I had my doubts that such a successful career could be so easily explained, but this author pulled it off in spades. I'm looking at real estate investment in an all new way after reading this book. I plan to share it with my next generation young adults so they will know what to look for (and what to avoid) as they begin their property buying careers. Thanks for sharing your secrets, Kristin!

William Bierce | Award-winning attorney and best-selling author of *Smarter Business Exits*

INVESTPRENEUR

I Can. I Will. Watch Me!

Real Estate Lessons for the Determined Investor

Kristin Cripps

Leaders
Press

Leaders
Press

Cover by Dalchand Sharma.

ISBN: 978-1-943386-85-7 (pbk)
ISBN: 978-1-943386-86-4 (ebook)
Library of Congress Control Number: 2020913107

This book is dedicated to anyone and everyone who made me laugh if I was stressed or having a rough day, who encouraged me when others thought I was in over my head, and who looked up to me and said if anyone could do it, I could. For those who helped me up when I fell, for those who knew that the walls were just protection and tunneled their ways through. Thank you for every smile, every chuckle, every wink, every tear, every hug. I love you all dearly and am so honoured to share my time on this earth with you.

Join Kristin as she shows you how to go even further building your REAL ESTATE EMPIRE with her exciting online course:

BUILD YOUR
empire

Contents

Introduction 1

Part 1 Introduction to Real Estate Investing 7

Part 2 Preparing for That First Purchase....................... 21

Part 3 Designing Your New Investments 57

Part 4 What to Do with Your Real Estate...................... 81

Part 5 Landlording 107

Part 6 Masterclass 155

Part 7 What's Next... 173

Conclusion.. 179

Acknowledgments.. 185

About the Author 187

Introduction

Ninety percent of all millionaires become so through owning real estate. More money has been made in real estate than in all industrial investments combined. The wise young man or wage earner of today invests his money in real estate.

—Andrew Carnegie

Andrew Carnegie knew what he was talking about: he led the expansion of the steel industry and became one of the wealthiest Americans in history. He passed in 1935 (the year my grandma was born), and during the last eighteen years of his life, he gave away 90 percent of his money, which was a staggering $350 million, guesstimated to be around $65 billion in our day.

Did you know the US has the highest number of millionaires in the world? According to Credit Suisse, US millionaires top with 18.6 million and comprise 40 percent of the world's high-net-worth individuals. There are just over 327.2 million people in the States, according to the US Census Bureau, which means that over 5.5 percent of US citizens are millionaires. Canada had 1.3 million millionaires in 2018, according to Credit Suisse, which means that 3.5 percent of the folks in my home base are millionaires. Ps it is 2020 when I am typing this but for some reason I can't find anything newer then 2018.

High fives all around to Canada, the States, and all you hustling-and-not-afraid-to-get-your-hands-dirty folks!

When I was in my early twenties, which was like a few months ago (wink, wink), it seemed that everyone I knew wanted to be a dental hygienist, massage therapist, or bartender. Now it seems everyone wants to be in real estate. Way to go, investors of the world!

So why are *you* curious about becoming a real estate investor or house flipper?

Perhaps you've watched all the shows on HGTV, like *Masters of Flip, Fixer Upper, Flip or Flop, Love It or List It*, or maybe you're more of a *Slice* fan and binge *Million Dollar Listing*, like your life revolves around it—no judgements. You like the idea of making money and earning passive income while your renters pay down your mortgage. Cheers to that—clink, gulp, happy sigh! You're creative and have the designer's natural green thumb, or you've ran your numbers and can afford to just hire it out. Bottom line, you see the potential in investing and want your share.

But are you afraid to make the wrong decision? Are you afraid to pick the wrong property? Concerned you might buy in the wrong neighborhood? Worried that your tenants won't pay you? Or even worse, perhaps the tenants will wreck your house?

I get it. These are all valid points. Much of the general public (and even me in the past) has these very same concerns. Unfortunately, these concerns are also what keeps people from entering the real estate investment market and, in most cases, having true financial freedom.

But think about this: even when markets crash and people walk away from their homes, they still pay rent to live *somewhere*. Instead of having five applications for a property, landlords will have eighty-five applications because they don't have to sell during a market crash. Plus, they often scoop up a bunch of additional properties at lower prices and know the value can only go up.

It's all too common when getting started in the real estate business to be a worrywart—but that's precisely when you need to think of the bigger picture and your endgame. The small things you worry about won't matter in the long run. I hope it helps you to know that you're not alone and that many new investors share the same fears and concerns you have. Whenever I face a decision, my trick is to ask myself if this decision is going to matter in three years.

For example, will it matter in three years if I had to unexpectedly purchase a $700 dishwasher and pay a plumber $200 to hook it up in one of my rentals?

Nope.

Is it going to matter in three years if a basement flooded in a rental and I had to submit a claim through my insurance so they can cover the lost rent and repairs?

Nope.

Here's a quick summary of the pros and cons of buying real estate for investments and/or flips. You'll see that no matter your concerns, you're in good company:

Pros

1. You know that nine out of ten millionaires become so through real estate.
2. Your renters will pay down your mortgage(s).
3. Your property (depending on the area and the homework you did) will go up in value.
4. You can work less (or not work at all) once you have more passive cash flow coming in.
5. You can use your extra money for whatever you want (I like to visualize myself with a credit card, like a kid in a candy store, thinking over what I would buy).
6. Bonus points if you're handy and can save money by not contracting repairs out to other people! (At first, of course—because once you're financially free, this won't be the best use of your time.)

Cons

1. You buy the wrong house.
2. You get in over your head.
3. You can't afford the repairs on the home.
4. You have nightmare tenants.
5. You can't afford to put a pool in your own backyard because you put it into a rental property and renovations there instead.
6. You already have a career and may not have time to be a landlord and do the maintenance and upkeep.

Over the years, many people have asked me how I went from being a massage therapist, server, and bartender to creating a successful real estate empire. I'm honoured to be asked and have dedicated the next chapter of my life to showing others how to do what I do.

It's not that difficult, I promise!

Recently, I became super inspired to help others live their best lives when I was approached more and more by women who said they enjoyed knowing a local female who is doing so well in business. They'd add that you travel and seem to enjoy all the world has to offer—and then they often add some version of "but is not with a spouse." They say, "you did it on your own," and many of their eyes light up. I love the excitement they have and want to show them how they can have the same opportunities.

I'm not saying that there's anything wrong with having a spouse (in the future, I will be with a kick-ass someone), but just because you're single doesn't mean you can't live an empowered breathtaking life! The more complete you are in all aspects, the better kind of partner you're going to attract. In the meantime, for when you find that person, isn't it fun to have the funds to do whatever you want whenever you want?

Real estate investing is an excellent way to fulfill your dreams and have that extra cash!

As you read this book, you're going to learn how to be fearless about getting into the real estate game. Despite what you might think right now, I'm going to show you that it's really quite manageable. Real estate investment can work for anyone at any age, but you have to know what you're doing.

(And after you finish this book, you will know *exactly* what to do!)

Keep reading for your guide to get into the game and make your mark.

Whether you dive in, cannonball, backflip, or belly flop, you're ready.

So let's do this!

Part 1

Introduction to Real Estate Investing

Don't wait to buy real estate. Buy real estate and wait.
—Will Rogers, actor

Who is Kristin Cripps?

The first and most important thing I want you to know about me is that I'm just a regular person. I don't have an advanced degree. I didn't grow up around money. I've never even been to university, yet I was a millionaire by my thirtieth birthday.

I don't want you to think it takes lottery winnings, inheritance, stocks, bonds, and portfolios to hit it big with your investments. Real estate investing can be quite straightforward and achievable by anyone willing to put in a bit of elbow grease. You don't even need to put in a lot of grease, just a bit.

When I was young, my first bank card came with a little piggy bank for pennies, nickels, dimes, and quarters. My parents modeled and encouraged saving, but they wouldn't say, "Spend 40 percent, save 50 percent for university, put away 10 percent for charity." They didn't break it down like that for me, but they did emphasize the importance of saving money.

My stepmom taught me a general guideline that I used for years: strive to meet all your bills for the month with one weeks' pay.

She said that if it takes you three weeks to make your car payment, rent or mortgage, utilities, and groceries, then if you run into financial trouble, you will quickly fall behind. So I never dipped into my savings account, and as I watched it grow, it became a great incentive for me to keep on saving. I always put my excess earnings in savings, and that's where my extra jobs came in handy. If I had only been massaging and not bartending in the evenings, for example, it would've been extremely hard to save money. I might've saved $10,000 in five years instead of saving $85,000 by the time I was nineteen years old.

Yes, you read that right: I saved $85,000 before I was twenty years old.

How? You may ask.

I worked three jobs at a time. I massaged during the day. I served tables at a steakhouse during the early evenings, and I tended bar every evening into the wee hours of the night. I didn't take a day off for a long time. Two days of this schedule paid my bills for the month, and I banked the rest, following my stepmom's advice.

I never thought about investing in anything at first. Luckily, I didn't spend it on a car (okay, only twice). As I made money, I didn't want to leave it at my house because I worried that somebody would take it, or I'd spend it on something stupid. So I kept socking that cash away in a separate bank account.

How did you get into real estate investing?

I bought my first house when my friend told me that my rent cost more than her mortgage. If she hadn't said that to me, I have no idea at what age I would have considered real estate, if ever. Thankfully, she made that statement to me—a light bulb went off—and I became curious and did some investigation.

I've always had a "bit" (insert wink here) of a shopping problem. But I wouldn't just buy things like clothes. One, I didn't need more clothes. Two, they were going to go out of fashion the next season. And three, purchasing something physical like a house seemed more logical to me, so I aimed to invest most of my savings in real estate.

I bought a townhouse at the age of nineteen without giving it too much thought. It was a three-bedroom, three-bathroom middle townhouse, with an unfinished walkout basement. Plus, it was dark, and since it wasn't an end unit, there were no side windows. Many times since then (and I'll share more about how to fix funky houses in later chapters), I've added extra windows to homes, made them bigger, done additions, or knocked them down completely. I didn't do much renovation in that unit other than rookying the basement to be finished and throwing on a coat of paint or two.

Aside from the townhouse itself, the neighborhood didn't work for me either. The people to the left of me filled their backyard with sunflowers. Three single guys lived on my right, and when they each had their kids over, they were excellent. But the rest of the time, it was 24/7 spring break. Everyone was partying and passing out on the lawn and front steps. It was not ideal.

Four months later, I put up for sale the home where I naively thought I would live my whole life. There are tons of lessons, tricks, and strategies in real estate. It took me a bit to learn how to make money in real estate, and I didn't know any of those lessons on my first purchase. (After reading this book, the same won't be true for you!) See, I wanted to keep the house as a rental, but I asked for advice from the wrong people and chickened out when I heard their dire warnings.

If only I would have held onto that townhouse! The next owners were able to capitalize on the profits that I was too afraid to go for. Today, that home is worth $275,000 more than I had sold it for, and if I would have sold it three years ago, it was worth even more!

I first considered getting into real estate as a career in my twenties. During the eight years I spent massaging and nine years bartending, I knew I wanted to do something else. I was looking for something to study so I could get out of the whole rat race. I used to call massaging mind-numbing, and bartending soul-draining, but I hadn't decided on a direction or career yet. I'd taken five introduction courses to interior decorating and design, but one of my teachers told me I wouldn't be able to work during the three-year program.

I said, "What do you mean I can't work? I bartended all the way through massage school."

She said, "The course load and the number of projects require so many hours that you physically won't have time to work."

That didn't wholly take the interior design education off the table for me. My thought was that I'm not typical, so I knew I could do it. But then another teacher asked if I knew that they had a 92 percent job placement rate. She said, "Well, the jobs are not at the places that you would think. They're not at some hip designer company or on TV. They're window changers or putting together furniture at IKEA, and I know that's not what you're looking for." That was true, so I was no longer interested in formal education for interior design.

Hmmm, what next now?

As time went on, I was personally buying and selling a lot of real estate. I thought I should get my license to save the 5 percent, which was the norm in my market at that time. But I never planned to do it for a living. I'd heard about some questionable incidents that happened to real estate agents and was concerned about my safety.

Real estate gradually became less of a hobby and more of a job as opposed to just saving me that bit of percentage. I didn't plan to become a realtor for profit but to save money, and I never thought I'd be voted number-1 agency in my city and have my team and brokerage. I did, however, carry mace around with me for the first three years in my bra, so in case there was ever a dicey or questionable situation, I was prepared.

To be honest, it wasn't like I got my license and immediately made boatloads of money. It was hard work at first, and I didn't make money for a long time, which is why I kept my other jobs until I was firmly established. I jumped with both feet into real estate investing when I felt the annoyance of seeing the market go up and up while counting the money I could have had. If only I had bought properties and stopped listening to other people scare me away from real estate investments and being a landlord sooner!

When I decided to get into investing, I looked at numbers, and once I noticed the math and the advantage, I started buying properties whenever I could—left, right, and centre. I looked at how much my mortgage was and how much rent was, and I could easily calculate the excess. You don't have to be a mathematician to calculate the win. If your mortgage is \$1,100 per month and the basement rents for \$975 and the upstairs for \$1,600, you're more than covering your bases by making \$1475 a month in addition.

For me, finding money to buy properties sometimes meant saving money by bartending or refinancing a home, or homes, I already owned. I did anything I could to keep buying more. I kept that small amount per house coming in each month and paid the mortgages on a fast track. I saw the rise in the communities as the purchase prices went up and up.

I would make automatic searches for myself for the specific homes I was looking for—if you're not a realtor, no sweat, as one can set you up for free on the exact same searches I was on. That way, I could be one of the first people there the day a house I wanted hit the market. I didn't want to wait until the weekend when someone else could snatch it up. Can you blame me? I couldn't afford purchases in the newer areas, so in the beginning, I searched in the older and often not the greatest areas that were usually sketchier and known for drugs.

If I found something that wasn't too bad (as some areas are just too bad that no amount of interior decorating can help) and saw that if I put in a nice kitchen or spruced up the place, it would rent. Depending on how bad the property was in the beginning, I could throw some stainless-steel appliances in, tear out the ratty carpet and put laminate down if need be, do some painting, add a second kitchen, and I was off to the races.

Buying houses intrigued me because they had three wins for me.

The first win was that I made a bit of money every month—not enough money to retire or go crazy, but enough to think to myself that it was better than nothing.

Second, the tenants pay down the principal (for mortgages, I always do rapid weekly or biweekly payment because it pays the mortgages off in fewer years). When you eventually sell, it's obviously beneficial to owe less and have more money in your pocket.

Lastly, the property goes up in value every year. Now I know this isn't the case everywhere, but it was where I was living and investing. Also, I love remodeling and decorating, so that gives me another outlet to my why. I can design, pick new bathrooms, flooring, and lighting to feed that addiction (it is an addiction, and they say the first step is admitting it. Done, admitted.) It's better to spend money on remodeling than clothes, I figure. (However, don't second-guess me, I can clothes shop with the best of them!)

Is investing in real estate doable for anyone?

You've just read my abbreviated story. However, the core message I want to share in this book is that *anyone* can build wealth with real estate investments—it's attainable if you take the proper action. Yes, there will be tiny road bumps (and I will be sharing some of my doozies), but they don't have to kill your journey unless you allow that to happen. The outcome far supersedes the little issues with being an investor. Plus, success in real estate can fuel your dreams, whatever those may be.

But before we discuss dreams, let's face reality.

Did you know that 25 percent of Canadians aged fifty-five to eighty have debt but no savings? According to the Sun Life Financial Survey, one in five of these retirees still have mortgage payments, and 66 percent still have credit card debt they can't pay off. Around 7 percent of these people have taken holidays they still haven't paid for, and 6 percent have renovations for which they still owe contractors or have paid for with lines of credit.

One-third of the people working in that age group said they were working because they had to, not because they wanted to. My grandma, Omi, worked until she was too out of it from her brain tumor to work anymore. Unfortunately, I was too young to show her financial freedom or spoil her with what I've eventually acquired, but that doesn't mean I can't help other people, including you!

Most people don't think about retirement at all, let alone plan for it. They hope someone will take care of them, whether that's the government or a family member. Why not set yourself up for life and have that cash flow for whatever you want— whenever you want? Because that's what investing in real estate can do for you.

Perhaps you worry that you don't have the funds to buy a rental property. This may be the case, at least right now. Maybe the bank won't lend to you due to poor debt-to-service ratio or poor credit, but there are still options. If you're waiting for a second house to land in your lap without any effort on your part, then you truly are dreaming. I am not someone who will lie to you and blow smoke up your ass and say, "Don't worry! If you're a good person and you *deserve* it, it will come to you."

There's always another job or two—or heck, who am I kidding? Fifty jobs!—to do if you want to get ahead financially. I'm not saying you have to take on a side hustle, but it will definitely help you fast-track your way to saving up for a real estate purchase. You can rent rooms in your house or short-term rent on Airbnb, VRBO, or whatever platform is popular where you live. Put an apartment above your garage, add a basement apartment, or divide part of your house you're not using.

Maybe you don't think being a landlord is for you. What if the tenants don't pay rent, or what if they trash the place?

Well, what if one day you need to go to a nursing home for special care, but you can't afford it? What if you need treatment for an ailment not covered by insurance? What if you haven't done anything you wanted to do in life because you haven't had the funds to do so? What then?

You will have held back on your dreams and comfort in later life because of your early fears! Fuck that!! Sorry but that deserves swearing.

My dad once gave me a book about fear. I read the back cover and knew it wasn't for me. (Sorry to waste your money, Dad. I should have given it to a library and not thrown it in the recycling bin.) I feel that what you put energy toward and think about becomes your reality, so I didn't want fear and scary situations to manifest in my life.

Being aware of fear is kind of like having a devil on one shoulder, an angel on the other, and someone asking you, "Which little figure has more power to win the decisions with you?" The winner is whichever one you feed more. The little devil or angel will get stronger and healthier, and those mindsets and patterns will become more and more ingrained in your psyche over time.

Getting over any fears that you won't be able to enter the investment game, that you're not smart or skilled enough to make money, that you don't know how to renovate may be the biggest hurdles you'll have to jump. But you can do it: real estate investment is for anyone!

Where do I start if I want to get into real estate investing?

You can watch YouTube videos and not pay one penny besides your data usage for all that knowledge. You can go to the library and read until the cows come home. You can approach successful local realtors and ask for mentoring. Buying that first home is likely the hardest step. But once you see what your investment is making for you, I promise that you'll wonder why you didn't do it sooner.

People ask me, "What are you going to do with your investments? Are you going to stop at ten houses? Or twenty houses?"

The answer is that I don't know. I don't have a plan to make an exact amount of money.

Some houses only earn me $100 to $300 monthly. My property in Toronto varies each month because it's a short-term rental. Some months it makes $9,000; some months it makes nearly $16,000. But it never makes less than $9,000, and that's after paying my mortgage!

For my Toronto house, I had to put $200,000 down. But with 5 percent down on a $300,000 house, you might only be making $115 to $300 back a month. It's incredibly unlikely that you will start making thousands of dollars each month off one property, so I want to be straight with you that there are steps to this ladder. So do you start smaller? Yes.

But eventually, you can buy another house, then another, and soon have the funds to buy something with an even greater return. But you can't jump straight to it, just like you can't jump to being an NFL sports star when you've never thrown a football before: you have to do the in-between stuff first. That's how much I don't know about football; I call it the in-between stuff, but I'm talking about practicing, drills, games—the process of year after year of being coached, improving, and pushing yourself.

Rents will continue to go up while your tenants pay your mortgage down. You can always refinance a property and pull that money out to buy another house. Let's say your first home is now making $300 a month. Maybe you have two more that are making $300 a month. You're getting more and more return. Maybe you can turn them into three units instead of two units and increase your income (more on that later).

What can investing in real estate do for me?

The simple truth is that investing in real estate can give you whatever you desire. (Part of me wants to say, well, maybe you can't buy a jet, but in reality, you can.)

Let's talk about the typical level for context here.

Real estate can pay off student debts, cars, homes, retire your parents, take you on adventures around the world, buy you clothes, rocks (*diamonds*, not rocks on the side of the road), allow you to donate to charities, start other companies, send kids to school (private, post-secondary, or both), supplement your income so you can leave jobs that may not be making you happy, buy boats, put in pools, buy cottages… I could go on forever.

Whatever your dreams, real estate investing can help you get there! But—and this is key—you must know your worth and not be afraid to invest in yourself.

For example, one client of mine said she wasn't going to Florida for a week or two over winter break because she didn't want to spend $1,000 to $1,800 on a vacation. I feel like we only remember our one life, whether we have more or not. So why not enjoy that life and not worry about things? Don't be an Eeyore!

How are you going to get anywhere if you're moping around like you're the most hard up person out there? It's guaranteed that somebody has it worse than you do, but it's also guaranteed that someone started in a better place than you. So be the best you can be, and don't think of where other people are, but rather conquer and stand proud!

It's never too late to break into the real estate investment game and make enough money for a comfortable retirement. If you're taking on a massive project that isn't going to see a return in your lifetime, ask yourself who will it help. Your kids? Your grandkids? Other family and friends? Perhaps even your favourite charity? If you want to leave your money to your family, then all the power to you. But what if you have things you haven't done yet? What if you would regret if you didn't do what you wanted before your number is up?

Go for it!

Keep reading and I will show you exactly how to make your mark by investing in real estate.

Part 2

Preparing for That First Purchase

Buying real estate is not only the best way, the quickest way,
the safest way, but the only way to become wealthy.
—Marshall Field, entrepreneur

Investing in real estate is not rocket science. I could be greedy
and pretend it's a closely guarded secret that has been passed
on by the gods to me and me alone, but that's not the case. As
long as you have the will and you're not an excuse maker, then
there's a way to succeed in real estate investing. You can put as
little as 3.5 percent (or in some cases, no money) down in the
States. So if you're still making excuses about how you can't buy
property, then enjoy your misery and bullheadedness because
you're the only one standing in the way of your opportunities.

How do I save up that first down payment?

We've all heard the statistics of the number of lottery winners
who declare bankruptcy within five years of hitting the *winning*
numbers. Many professional athletes lose all their hard-earned
income once their high-paying career is over because they don't
save and invest. If they had a dollar, they'd spend a dollar; if they
had $100, they'd spend $100. What makes us think if they have
$10 million, they won't spend that as well? In reality, a lot of
people rack up $115 or even more for every $100 they earn.
We're in a time of severe overspending.

End of lecture.

Oh, wait, one more: you need to be in the habit of saving at least 10 percent of your pay.

You might say, "You don't know my pay, and it's impossible to live off what I make, let alone save anything." Okay, then can you save one percent? I bet you can! Then you can up it to 2 percent when you're ready. You might be surprised by what you can save. Set up an auto-withdrawal to come out of your bank account so you don't notice the savings. When you see it accumulating in a separate account, it will inspire you to save even more.

As I mentioned, I saved my down payment working many hours bartending. Massaging paid my bills, such as my car, utilities, food, and clothing, while bartending was my extra for travel, shopping, and investments. That was my plan. What could you do to save for a down payment?

Here are a couple of ideas to save a down payment:

- ❏ Get another job—or heck, get two jobs, preferably with tips or commission.

- ❏ Rent out rooms in your home to a long-term roommate or a short-term renter even if you don't own the home.

- ❏ Rent the basement apartment—or better yet, you live in the basement apartment and rent out the upstairs since it will bring in more money per month.

- ❏ Rent out your place on a short-term rental site such as Airbnb or VRBO when you're away on vacation or visiting family or friends overnight.

- ☐ Try waitressing.

- ☐ Be an Uber driver.

- ☐ Deliver pizza.

- ☐ Put an ad online and offer to tutor those learning to speak another language and charge hourly for your services. (Of course, only if you speak another language, duh. Just shy of half of Canadians weren't born in Canada. What do you think is the percentage of them that can speak another language? Pretty friggin high!)

- ☐ Tutor a child to help before a big exam.

- ☐ Maybe you're good at editing videos.

- ☐ If you're really good at social media sites, you can manage someone else's account.

- ☐ Get paid as an influencer to sponsor things.

- ☐ Walk dogs.

- ☐ Be a personal trainer.

- ☐ Gain a following on a social platform, and see if you can get any brand deals to show their product.

- ☐ …you get the idea.

Use your imagination, people!

Don't worry. In due time, you will have the extravagant things by making the sacrifices now! For example, if you work nine to five, think about what you can do in the evenings or on the weekends. I get it, you're tired. But you don't have to maintain this schedule forever, just until you've saved what you need. It doesn't have to be seven days a week. Just do what you can, and know that the more you do now, the less you will have to do later. You might as well get it out of the way. Little things add up, and everything you do along the way affects the endgame. Don't you want a kick-ass endgame? If you don't care and are fine living from paycheck to paycheck, then you don't need to finish reading this book. All the best to you.

But if you do care, there are *so many ways* to earn extra money. No matter where you live or what you do, there's money to be made. If you sit at home and pick your nose, or post to Instagram or TikTok—or whatever you do at home—you're losing money. (Unless you have a massive following and are building a successful brand with sponsorships and kickbacks, of course.)

I forget who told me back in the day that TV is an "income suppressor." Granted, there's the odd educational show, but most likely, that's not the juicy drama you're addicted to. You might as well look out the window and watch the dollars fly away. I know it's kind of blunt and rude of me to say, but I don't sugarcoat things—sorry. If you're looking for someone to stroke your ego and say that's not fair and you should just be handed everything, you're in the wrong place.

Now is the time to educate yourself about the types of mortgages available to you. Do you qualify for a loan at this point? Maybe you jump around jobs too often, or you're self-employed and unable to prove income. It's always good to be familiar with your situation and know what you could improve to make yourself a better candidate for a bank's loan/lending department.

Fix what you can on your credit as soon as possible to help lenders work with you. As you work on saving your down payment, clean up the other areas of your financial life by paying bills on time or early, not keeping your credit cards teetering at their max, not going into overdraft, and paying off loans before they're due.

What are the minimum down payments required for US loans?

In the States, it's easier to get a mortgage than it is for Canadians. In the States, citizens have the option of taking advantage of no-money-down loans or 3.5% interest rates. US insurance is different from Canada as well. Canadians must have an insured mortgage if putting less than 20% down. During the odd time when US citizens must have an insured mortgage, they can cancel it the next day whereas Canadians are not allowed to exercise that option.

Those conditions make it easier for US citizens to get mortgages. Now I'm not trying to be Canada vs. the States—or anyone vs. anyone for that matter—but stop making excuses regardless of where you live and instead look into what you need to do, investigate the rules, and get ready to buy. Rules and regulations are constantly changing, and new programs are continuously coming out, so check with a local expert for what would work best with your situation.

Assuming you don't have a money tree in your backyard, you will need a mortgage. The following are the loans currently offered in the US with minimum down payments.

Be sure to check which one works for you and what might have changed or been added since I wrote this book.

Conventional Loans

- ❑ It has a 5 percent down payment.
- ❑ It's available for loans up to $417,000.
- ❑ If the amount is larger than $417,000, the down payment can be as low as 10 percent.

FHA Loans

- ❑ It has a 3.5 percent down payment.
- ❑ It's available for one to four family homes
- ❑ It typically carries lower interest rates than conventional mortgage loans.
- ❑ Those with a credit score below 600 can qualify.

VA Loans

- ❑ This loan is for current or former members of the military.
- ❑ No money down is required.
- ❑ If interest rates drop after you've been in your house for a while, look into VA streamline refinance loans (IRRRL), which can reduce your rates significantly at a lower cost than a conventional refinance loan.

USDA Loans

❏ This is for rural or outer suburban areas.

❏ It's a federally insured loan designed to bring housing within reach for lower-income country dwellers

❏ Unlike FHA and VA loans, USDA loans are direct loans made by the USDA.

Conventional 97 Loans

❏ It has a 3 percent down payment for a maximum LTV (loan to value) of 97 percent.

❏ It is backed by Fannie Mae.

Piggyback Loans

❏ These are two loans taken at the same time to cover a substantial portion of a home's purchase price.

❏ This is used by those who have less than 20 percent to put down on a home.

❏ It requires a down payment

❏ A common scenario is to make a 10 percent down payment and take a first mortgage for 80 percent of the purchase price and a piggyback loan for the remaining 10 percent.

HomeReady Mortgage

❏ It has a 3% percent down payment.

❏ It's a private mortgage insurance you can terminate once you reach 20 percent equity.

❑ Gifts, grants, Community Seconds mortgages and cash on hand are all allowable sources of down payment and closing cost funds.

❑ You need a credit score of at least 680.

Home Possible Advantage

❑ Purchase and refinance (no cash-out) mortgage program is offered by Freddie Mac to borrowers who do not own any other residential property (some exceptions apply).

❑ At least a 3 percent down payment is required.

❑ It requires mortgage insurance but can be canceled once 18 to 25 percent equity established

❑ At least a credit score of 660 is needed.

Good Neighbor Next Door

❑ This is for eligible teachers, law enforcement officers, firefighters, and emergency medical technicians.

❑ Eligible buyers can purchase a HUD-owned single-family home for 50 percent off the appraised value of the home.

❑ Down payment is as low as $100, and the buyer must live in the home for at least three years.

❑ The discounted amount is represented by a second mortgage that is forgiven after the occupancy requirement is completed.

❑ If you don't complete the occupancy requirement, you will be responsible to repay the second mortgage on a prorated basis.

Guaranteed Rate

- ❑ A 3 percent down payment is required, and Guaranteed Rate will gift up to 2 percent of the purchase price with a $7,500 maximum.

- ❑ Minimum FICO score is 680, and the loan may not exceed conforming loan limits.

- ❑ Borrower's DTI (debt to income ratio) may not exceed 45 percent.

- ❑ Income and property type limits apply, and homeownership counseling is required of first-time buyers.

What kinds of loans are available to Canadians?

Canada doesn't offer the above options, so most people will need a 5 percent down payment to take out a loan. However, there are different grants available. Currently, they're offering a grant with no interest or payments for 5 percent down for new buyers if it's a resale home and 10 percent if it's a new build.

Buyers may, however, have to pay it back when they sell. If the house goes down in value, they don't have to pay it at all. If it goes up significantly, they must pay more (but they could pay it before it sells if they came into some money—perhaps from the basement apartment they've added or rooms they've rented on Airbnb or taking on a second job). Also, the 5 percent grant has to be in addition to the 5 percent the buyer has already saved, so it's like a top-up to 10 or 15 percent from your saved up 5 or 10 percent.

Genworth, one of three insurers for mortgages in Canada, did a 2019 study on first-time buyers. The study indicated that 33 percent of buyers were less than thirty years old, 36 percent were between thirty and forty, and the remainder were older. Three-quarters of new buyers were born in Canada, and the rest were immigrants. What buyers rated as most important to least important was as follows:

- ❑ price
- ❑ safe neighbourhood
- ❑ size of home
- ❑ style/design of the home
- ❑ value as an investment
- ❑ proximity to work

Over 60 percent of first-time buyers said they thought house prices would increase in the next twelve months, and 48 percent said they would rather have a more expensive, smaller home closer to work than a cheaper one that was farther away. However, since that survey was conducted before the COVID-19 pandemic, buyers may instead opt for homes further away now as they adjust to working from home or finding new jobs altogether.

How much should I put aside besides my down payment?

If you plan to live in the home, you can get away with having approximately $10,000 on hand. Depending on the purchase price, you could need $5,000 for land transfer tax, $1,500 for lawyer fees, and $3,500 for basic furnishings. That's a great start.

Land transfer tax/transfer taxes will run you about 1 percent, which is a good general rule of thumb. However, there's a city in Canada where the percentage is double, so check the area where you plan to purchase to be sure. There are also often grants for first time buyers that forfeit your land transfer tax, so see if that applies where you live before you think you need that extra $10,000.

Usually, when buying property, you can expect to pay between $1,200 to $1,800 in lawyer's fees, but $1,500 is the norm.

If you plan to replace the appliances that come with the property or make other upgrades, you should plan to have more on hand. I've known people to pay over $10,000 just for appliances, and I've known people to spend ridiculous amounts of money on couches. So the amount of extra funds needed on hand depends on your budget and plans and what you feel is "necessary" in your home.

If you plan to rent out the home on a short-term basis, then you will need to fully stock the unit with furniture, kitchenware, linens, toiletries, and so forth. How much you will need for this purpose depends on your budget and whether you are a cheap or extravagant shopper. I've known people to furnish rentals from garage sales, online deals, and through "used" platforms— and others who spend $10,000 for a sectional couch.

Five thousand dollars is a healthy buffer zone to have set aside, but if you have less, you could still make things jive. I can count on one hand how many big-ticket items I've had to replace in all my transactions and rentals, as customarily, I spend just $500 or less per year. For example, I recently got a call about a faulty dishwasher. The repairman said I needed a water inlet valve, and including his hourly, the repair was still less than $200. The last time I had to do any work at that unit was about four years ago, but I like to be overcautious as opposed to being short-changed for issues.

Who pays the real estate agent's commission, title search, and insurance on a sale?

Traditionally, the seller pays both sides of commission, but there is the odd buyer's agent who wants the buyers to pay a fee. I've never run across it in Canada, but I have heard of transactions like this in the US.

The title search is included with our lawyer's fees in Canada, and insurance is paid monthly on a house. One hundred dollars per home per month is a good guideline. The odd time, you will pay $140 a month, but it all comes down to the house. For example, if the home is siding over brick, the insurance will cost a little bit more.

Basically, your insurance will base it on how much they think they'll need to pay to replace the whole home and then equate that by a rate they use to reach a monthly amount.

Are there faster ways to pay down my mortgage?

One of the ways I work on paying down mortgages faster is by making weekly or biweekly payments. Let's say, your mortgage is $1,172 per month for twenty-five years. If you pay $600 every other Friday, then it will cut down your mortgage by four years, so now you only have to pay it for twenty-one years instead of twenty-five! If you pay $300 every week, or $302 every Friday, then it will be seventeen or eighteen years before you pay it off. Because I was making money every night bartending, I could cut years off my mortgage by paying more frequently than once a month, so I always paid weekly mortgage payments.

I didn't know anything about mortgages at first, but I soon learned to pay down the mortgages with every one of my investments. Let's say, you have a $300,000 mortgage. Approximately (it's not so cut and dry), one half goes toward principal, and half goes toward interest. Sometimes it's even more, like 75 percent goes toward interest with only 25 percent put toward the principal. Biweekly payments don't change the principal, but the payments do change the amount you pay in interest because you pay it off early and make your term shorter.

You can choose biweekly or rapid biweekly mortgage payments and save a lot of money. With biweekly, you divide how many months and weeks are in a year and pay every other week. With rapid biweekly, it's divided using fewer months in the year. Let's say they calculate payments using ten months in the year instead of twelve, hence raising your payments. I've always done rapid biweekly, or weekly if it's available. Not all mortgage institutions offer biweekly payments because they want to collect as much interest as possible.

What should I do when I'm ready to buy?

Once you've got your down payment sorted and discovered which kinds of loans you can qualify for, then it's time to consider a few scenarios.

The very first thing you need to do before buying is to determine what kind of investor you're going to be. Plan way ahead of time if you know you'll be living in the property, flipping it, or keeping it to rent out on a short or long-term basis.

Are you going to buy one house where you reside and rent out a room? Will you rent out a separate basement apartment in your home? Or will you buy a property in addition to the one where you will live? Will the new home be down the street from yours or across the country or the ocean? Will you keep it or flip it? Will you rent it long or short-term? Should you buy one or two homes if you can afford it, or pay the mortgage down on one instead?

If you plan to flip, and you're considering a house an hour from a city (and maybe a small city at that), the number of days on the market before selling is going to be incredibly high and will probably not be your best move. However, if you've chosen to do short-term rentals, then a beautiful cottage an hour from the hustle and bustle of a major metropolitan city (after you've considered your competition) is probably safe to buy.

Which type of style to buy?

If you're intending to rent long-term, do you buy a one-unit home or multiple units? If you buy multiple units, check for adequate parking. Are the bedrooms located directly on top of each other, or is one living room right over one renter's bedroom? These are things to consider should one renter be sleeping when another is having friends over or kids running around in the living room.

What style should you purchase? What makes sense as a rental, and what doesn't? How do you leave your heart and emotions out of it? You need to be like those guys on TV playing in poker tournaments. You can't let the other side know how you feel about the property or which cards you're holding. You can't have attachments and must be able to walk away if the pricing and conditions don't align. Don't overpay because you have your heart set on a property—that has bad news and poor investing written all over it.

Type of neighbourhood

Is the home you're looking at the nicest one on the street or block, or are the other homes similar? Is the one you're looking at the eyesore of the subdivision? Will the neighbours petition you to do something with that hot mess property of yours?

I once lived in a home that I owned for eleven years in an area divided into two types of sections.

One was prim and proper with teeny Yorkies and Chihuahuas parading by on their owner's leashes. Those owners petitioned if your gardens weren't up to par. They vacuumed their lawns in the summer to rid the lawn of the remnants of the salt from the winter months so it wouldn't kill their grass.

The other area was completely different. If you hadn't cut your grass in ten years, nobody cared. Everyone had big dogs, and most were running around the neighborhood off leash.

Look at the homes in the area. If the homes are of equal or better value than the one you're considering, you're on the right track. Don't buy the nicest home on the street or in the neighbourhood, as the others will pull you down and will be happy to do so, which is kind of like life: flush those out who are not serving, motivating, and pushing you to be the best version of yourself.

Now some neighbourhoods look divey but are known to be "up and coming." Just make sure that's the truth if that's the story you're being told. Check with the township or city about the plan for the neighbourhood. You might be surprised by how many plans they have on file for the future and which ones are approved.

For example, is the city putting in a recreation centre or a library near the neighborhood? Is an institution such as a university dumping money into a nearby project? This often spikes home values. If everything is boarded up, and no one wants to buy, then that's obviously not good. Maybe zoning is changing from residential to factory use.

Make sure you check out the neighbourhood and house where you are interested at all hours of the day. Let's say, you drive by at 2:00 pm, and everything is all roses and sunshine. But if you return at 5:30 pm, and it becomes a ghost town because the sunshine and roses have left and now it's a rough area, steer clear.

Also, go on the weekend and see what the neighbours are doing. Are they playing ball with their kids and riding bikes in the neighbourhood? Or are they drinking in their garage with the door up and whooping, hollering, and staggering around?

Neighbours can be deal breakers, so definitely check the property and neighborhood you're considering during different hours of the day and on weekends. There's nothing worse than trying to have an open house on a Saturday afternoon when the neighbours are meeting with their local motorcycle gang in their driveway during the two-hour time slot you have to sell your investment property or flip.

I made an offer on a home in Bali after touring around on the back of my agent's scooter during the day. We were together from around 11:00 am to 4:00 pm, so we weren't navigating a busy rush hour in the streets. However, and most importantly, the house he showed me—that I adored, loved, and offered on—sat next door to a live rock nightclub.

Yes, I said *live*—not a DJ with a MacBook, but full on drums, electric guitars, screaming, and heavy metal head-banging kind of music seven nights a week. Conveniently, I wasn't told about the club, and even when I asked about the neighbours, I was told it was a restaurant that closed at 7:00 pm every evening. After some digging and checks on the sound, I definitely passed on that house. Always visit at different times of the day and week! Bullet dodged!

Listing history

Check out how many times the home has changed hands. Has it been listed and sold a million times? Why aren't people staying? What is it that they are experiencing or noticing about the home or area that is keeping them from staying at the property?

Check how long the house has been listed for, and if it's a long time, then dig into why that might be the case. Do homes in the neighbourhood have multiple offers on the first day and typically sell for over the asking price? If so, at what price? Is the one you're looking at sitting stagnant in relation to those other homes? Is it because it's priced too high, or does it have an odd layout, an unusable lot, or is right next to the plaza with the gas station?

Just because you may be able to get it cheaper because it has a "stigma" attached to it, it may not be worth it. There are certain things you can change, but a bad location is not one of them. Be careful because you could have just as much or more trouble selling it in the future.

Amenities

If you're planning to short-term rent a cottage, check how far it is from the highway. Is it near a gas station, convenience store, or grocery store in case your guests want to buy something locally such as firewood or ice? If your rental is in a metropolitan city centre, can your guests easily walk to amusements? What about grocery stores, restaurants, and bars? If you're doing room rentals, there is little chance they'll cook in the kitchen, so most guests will likely want to purchase something in the vicinity.

If you're considering a property for longer rental, know that a one or two-bedroom will probably rent to a young couple. So what is the relation to the highway? Do they commute? They probably won't care much about a yard, so don't pay $50,000 extra for some grand yard when it may only get you $40 more a month in rent. Does the apartment look nice enough that they would rather live there than with their parents?

If there are more than two bedrooms, most likely the renters will have kids, so you'll need to consider the proximity to local schools. What about a bus stop? If they have a tween or teen who wants to go to a friend's house or take a part-time job, they'll probably want to take a bus. Is there a park nearby? They'll care more about the yard than other types of renters, but the yard doesn't have to be excessive.

Types of renters

It's harder to rent multiunit houses when tenants have kids, as sometimes they'll ask who lives in your other apartments as they may be uncomfortable with the whole "stranger" thing. If the other tenants access their unit through the backyard where their kids may be playing, this could be an issue.

Couples don't seem to mind this arrangement and often become friends. However, they usually don't want to rent an apartment below toddlers or kids who will naturally be running around upstairs in their apartment. The families with kids usually find that basement apartments are too tight for them.

These reasons are why I tended to find my success in one and two-bedroom multiplexes, but you need to test your area and do your research. I've always had my rentals in Toronto (home to 2.7 million people), Barrie (153,000) or one hour north of Barrie, but never further. My luck has been in city centres and cottages. I like to be driving distance from my rentals (even though I considered that property in Bali that didn't come together.)

Should I look for real estate in city centres?

Part of jumping into the real estate game is considering your scenario around where to get started. City centres are going to offer both pros and cons, depending on what you determine to be your target market. They're most likely going to be priced higher, but that means your returns will be higher as well.

Pros (for short-term rentals)

❑ City centres are often more desirable for tourists—especially foreign travelers.

❑ You'll have a lower vacancy rate.

❑ You will have a property in the city centre should you need a date night.

❑ There will be a wide arrangement of cleaning people to reset your unit between guests.

Cons (for short-term rentals)

❑ These properties usually cost more.

❑ You'll have more competition with other people also renting short-term.

❑ You may not get as much as you had hoped for unless you've done your research.

❑ You may be in a condo that does not allow short-term rentals or changes after you become an owner—then you'll need to sell, and a bunch of other owners might also sell at the same time, and you could lose money. (My metropolitan city unit is freehold, so there are no condo fees. I don't want other individuals or people on a committee to tell me what I can and can't do with my property.)

❑ Parking can be an issue. Most people staying will fly in and not have a car, but if they do, where will they park? Will they expect parking to be provided?

Pros (for long-term rentals)

❑ Tenants will probably stay longer due to the convenience of public transit.

❑ Tenants can walk to movies, shops, restaurants, or beaches.

❑ There's less chance they will party.

❑ Value often goes up at a healthy rate if it's a prosperous city.

Cons (for long-term rentals)

❑ It will probably be your most expensive mortgage, and you don't even get to live there and enjoy it.

❑ There's more purchase competition from local people and investors from your country and overseas if you have picked an increasing market.

❑ You could have issues with tenants, who often have more rights than the landlord.

Should fixer-uppers be cheaper?

I'm sure you agree that the point of a fixer-upper is to buy low, fix it up, and make a healthy profit. Because I love decorating so much, refurbishing fixer-uppers feeds and fuels that creative side of me, so it's a win for my mind. Some people can't look past the bad layout, ugly wallpaper, or even the furniture (you are *not* buying the furniture) and therefore can't see the potential of the property. This works out for me and you who enjoy the fixer-upper game because, then, there's less buying competition.

When considering a fixer-upper, it's even more important and essential to become familiar with both your bottom-line budget and maximum purchase price and other costs as early as possible. You need to be savvy enough to know that when you get a quote such as $80,000 for a roof or $30,000 for a furnace, you understand if that's a good deal, or you're being ripped off. And if you get those quotes in this example, you are being ripped off, but I've seen it done. Sometimes contractors are so busy or don't want to drive out to a certain location, so they will quote a ludicrous price tag on a quote, assuming the customer will say no. But if they say yes, then they say it is worth it for them.

But don't be afraid to let your inner design maven run wild. You could buy houses that have coloured counters, blue and pink carpets, and so forth. I once listed a house that sat forever and ever. All the agents at the office used to bug me, "Did you sell the Barney house yet?"

It was called the Barney house because the flooring in the house was ridiculous. One room was maroon, one green, one blue, and one red. You get the gist. We pulled the listing, and the owner replaced the carpets for a cost of $4,000. Then we relisted for $15,000 more, accepted $5,000 under asking, and—voilà—The Barney house became a distant memory.

Now someone like you could have seen the potential in that house, bought it for less, put in the $4,000, and been ahead of the game, but most people don't see the potential. Say, the bathrooms were ugly. If the budget didn't make sense or support adding complete new bathrooms, you could always make other changes. You could paint the cupboards and add new hardware and countertops. Splash the home with a five-gallon pail of one-colour neutral paint, and you have a facelift on the kitchen and a bright freshly painted home.

What primary parts of a house should I look at when considering whether to buy?

First, consider the neighbourhood at *all times* of the day. Then approach the house. How is the foundation and base? How many parking spaces are available? As you tally the positives and negative points on the house, consider what's changeable and what's written in stone.

Get detailed about your investment, and don't rush. As you become more skilled and experienced, you'll quickly know if it's a good deal or not. But in the beginning, you'll have a lot of money on the line, so you'll want to make sure you're being very precise and specific with your numbers: renovation costs, holding costs, solicitor charges, and extra emergency fund. You have all seen the shows where there's almost always unexpected costs, so don't say I didn't tell you so.

Take your time to decide if it's the right property and investment for you. If you're buying in a fast-paced market and don't have time to wait a week to run your numbers and do your homework, you can always offer on the home with conditions and then use that conditional period to do your homework. If it doesn't align and make sense, then you can back out, as opposed to waiting a week doing your homework and finding out that yes, it's a great deal, but someone else has already offered, and the sellers have accepted their deal. Get your foot in the door first!

The main things that buyers look at are the kitchen, bathrooms, and floors. This doesn't mean that they have to be done, because you may not have the money to make and improve the house. But check to see if the house has a good layout or potential for you to make improvements—look at the whole picture.

Kitchens

Can you spend $100,000 redoing a kitchen?

Absolutely—all day long!

Do you need to?

Absolutely not!

You can get a great kitchen at IKEA or some other similar kitchen-saver place. I have never spent over $5,000 for cupboards, and most times, I spend somewhere between $2,000 to $4,000. (PS: this does not count countertops or appliances, backsplash, or hardware.)

A couple of things to consider are the following: Is the kitchen open? Is it a galley? Is there a lot of storage space? How about counter space? Can you see the living room and the kids, or are you secluded in a dark, dingy corner of the house?

How is the lighting? Are you going to slice your finger off preparing dinner because the light has one bulb that's nowhere near the prep area? What about natural light? Is there one window that used to look outside, but then a garage was added, and now it looks in the garage? Natural light is important and always a bonus if you can add it if it doesn't already exist.

Depending on the price point you're in, you may be able to get away with painting the cupboards, changing the counter and appliances, or a complete overhaul might need to be done. You might have to remove walls or add support beams, or add quartz or granite countertops and all new cupboards and maybe an island.

Bathrooms

Consider the number of bathrooms. Is there only one bathroom in the house? You can imagine and perhaps have lived with one bathroom yourself and know how annoying it can be in the mornings trying to get ready for work or school. Is there a way to add an extra bath in a basement, an ensuite, or both? Is the master bedroom large and abuts a bathroom wall that you can make into an ensuite? Depending on their current state, bathrooms may need an update. If you can add a bathroom or two, praise the Lord and do it.

Floors

Chances are, you may have to redo the floors. In rentals and multiunits, carpet can be a good choice to muffle the noise if there are people below, but I don't like it for hygienic reasons. Renters may have kids, cats, dogs who spill, pee, or so forth. I prefer laminate for wear and tear and also had a phase of ceramic floors that look like hardwood. Although it's more labour to put ceramics down, unlike laminate, even if they get it soaking wet by a gallon of water or the dishwasher backs up, they won't curl. I have also used vinyl quite a bit for water reasons and just that they don't curl like laminate when they get overly soaked.

Does the house have hardwood flooring with outdated colouring? You could pay to have it sanded and redone. Is the style out-of-date such as a very skinny plank when wide is now in? Does it have parquet flooring? If you want me to dry heave like a child wanting french fries and being forced to have vegetables, then just show me parquet. Yuck! Depending on what your competition has and if the numbers all align and make sense, you might have to rip it out or go over the top with new flooring.

I had one tenant accidentally destroy my laminate. Right after moving out, he thought he would be nice and rent a steam cleaner to get the dog smell out of the house. He soaked the floors, which caused them to curl up, as I do when I cringe around rude people. I know he was just trying to be helpful, but they were not salvageable by any means.

If you go into any of my old flips, rentals, or renovations, you will find laminate flooring, but in my newer houses, you'll find vinyl or the ceramic floors that look like wood. I had a 105-pound dog for over twelve years, and I liked that he couldn't destroy the ceramic floors. Ceramics are cold on your feet and not great for your back, but I just wear flip-flops inside to add that extra cushion.

Natural light

Natural light is important. Is there a full door you can either make into a half-window or full-window door? Is there a wall that's screaming for a window? Are there dingy, claustrophobic basement windows that can be made safer and more aesthetically appealing to the space and hence larger?

When just starting out in real estate investment, what should I *not* buy?

My rule of thumb was always to seek a return of 10 percent or more, including the money I put down, the cash necessary for renovations, plus some extra because there were always hidden costs. I always asked if my rent would earn 10 percent or more making sure I was counting the utility bills, property taxes, insurance (and so forth), and still having that gain. If I was flipping it, I would look at "solds" in the neighbourhood because I planned on selling which made sense since the buyers would be doing the same, and they wouldn't want to overpay either. If you're buying for $300,000, putting $100,000 in, and the sales average $369,000 in the neighborhood, then that makes no sense. If the sales are $500,000 to $529,000, then you'll be laughing gleefully all the way to the bank when you flip the property.

I've bought houses knowing I would tear them down. I've blown roofs off, done major additions, built homes from scratch on vacant lots (or on lots where I tore the house down), and so forth. But I don't recommend that you buy fixer-uppers to bulldoze when you're starting. Get your feet wet first. I would advise that you pick something that is priced low because it needs a simple fix like a kitchen, bathroom, flooring, paint and/or smaller fixes. Until you're comfortable with costs, I wouldn't go for the big stuff because it's too overwhelming for a newbie—in most cases, it could get you into hot water if you don't calculate all your numbers correctly.

How do I recognize the point at which a house needs *too* much work?

You need to look at the full picture. For example, a friend called recently to talk about a century home that she was interested in buying. The home had knob-and-tube wiring, which was an early standardized method of electrical wiring used from about the 1880s to the 1940s. Plus it had a variety of other costly items that would need to be repaired.

She planned to spend $100,000 on renovations. However, with those kinds of projects, prices could quickly escalate to $200,000 or higher. As she has three children, I suggested that she steer clear of that one as so many things were needed to be done, and that was just what she could see. She knew there would be jobs like taking down a few walls, but I would bet my life that she would come across other things, such as asbestos and urea-formaldehyde, possibly termites, that would need to be remedied and would add considerable cost.

On another occasion, I showed a house to a client. She said, "I'd blow out this wall. Then I'd put all new windows. Then I would do this, this, and this." Her list was about $150,000 long.

I said, "But at the end of the day, it still has driveway parking for only one car and a dinky eighty-foot lot backing onto someone else's lot. Since they have a pool, do you really want to spend that money and hear cannonballs and 'Marco? Polo!' all day long?"

It would have been a good project if the lot had no neighbours behind, and the solds in the neighbourhood showed high value, but they didn't. I felt she wanted a project to get her creative juices flowing—but you can't change location. I suggested a hard pass.

Should I live in a property while I fix it up?

I suggest that maybe you split the unit into two so you can continue living there while improving the house and building more capital to purchase more real estate. I always move into the property, making it my primary residence so I could put the 5 percent down instead of 20 percent or 25 percent required for a non-primary residence when possible. Then I add a basement apartment or even a main floor apartment to cover my mortgage and add value. Then I either sell for profit or refinance and pull that money out, rent out the unit I was living in, and move to the next house—wash, rinse, repeat.

Depending on the size, some homes can even be split into three units—and the more units you can get out of a house, the more of a cash cow it is (moooo-la!). I have a friend who built a lovely 2800-square-foot bungalow house just two minutes outside of Barrie. First, he divided the basement into two 1,400-square-foot apartments. Then he put an apartment above the garage.

On this property, there was an old garage, so he sided and stoned it to match the new house and turned that into a little one-bedroom loft apartment. When it was finished, it equaled five units and is an official money maker—*yes, please!*

What are some desirable real estate investments that most people don't consider?

There are so many ways to make money in real estate! You don't have to only consider houses or apartments—there are many other options. For example, I have a property that's not great for a residence because it's in a rural/waterfront area, so I turned it into an Airbnb space.

I've only been doing short-term waterfront rentals for a little over a year and a half (before I always did long-term) and have had great success, but I worked my numbers before I made my decision. I learned that if I rented for seven weeks in the summer, the amount I earned covered me for the year. Any earnings on top of that was a bonus. I'd say there are less than twenty days a year that it's not rented so that seven weeks is definitely covered (cha-ching!).

I know of a barn not too far from where I live that can be rented for weddings, get-togethers, and corporate functions, and charges $15,000 a night on Fridays and Saturdays and rents other days for less. They have a tiny, shabby house they let the bride rent (she doesn't even get it for free), and people bring their own caterers, porta-potties, etc.

I remember when the owner used to rent it for $2,000 a night, and I thought that was insane. Then she just kept upping and upping her price, and the customers kept paying it. You just have to be creative and find a need for the community or area and fill it.

You could also buy a big factory space and convert it to studios for photography. People come with their photographer and take photos in a pretty space decorated by you, your contractor, or interior decorator. Then you can charge by the hour or the day.

I have also had a number of clients buy back splits, which are not so common in my region, but they liked them because they were often easy to turn into two and even three units. These five-level back splits also had plenty of means of egress (exit), so they were great for safety from a firefighter's point of view. You will often find them on slope sides, but the odd time on flat terrains. Tenants are quite far away from one another on the different levels, so sound and complaining of such are less of an issue.

Also, perhaps you can find a corner lot where off one side, you could either have an additional driveway for a secondary unit or a separate backyard. In the best-case scenario, the city or town will give you permission to add another dwelling or two. There are always ways around things, and sometimes you just have to get creative.

Sometimes the town or city will say no to a garage unless it's attached to the house. But then you might see a whole bunch of unattached garages around that area. Now don't throw them under the bus, but if you can say that other neighbours have unattached garages, ask how they got around the unattached rule. They might explain that the reason those other garages passed was that they are attached by the eaves trough (or gutters in the States) or attached by a deck railing or a breezeway.

Look for the loopholes, as I guarantee they exist. In that garage example, make an apartment, as a garage will net you peanuts over an actual living space. Also, if you're dealing with the city or town, make friends, not enemies; you will get a lot further by being nice to them than being a dick and them not giving you any breaks, letting any loopholes pass or so forth. Leave your ego at the door, or you may find that your file gets "conveniently" pushed to the bottom of the file. or "misplaced."

What should I look out for so I don't buy a money pit?

We've all heard the money pit stories: the kinds of houses that you buy, and the spending and improving just never ends. They fix one thing, and another thing breaks. It's like peeling an onion where each layer just leads to another layer of repair and expense. Here's a simple list of things to consider so you don't end up in a money pit.

Location

You've heard it a hundred times, at least: "Location, location, *location*." If you're looking or considering a home in a bad neighbourhood, don't do it. I know it's less expensive, and you can make it look so cute, but unless it's located in a transitioning, upcoming neighbourhood—which is not what I am referencing here—no quality tenant, long or short-term, will want to stay there.

Even if a short-term tenant is from out of town, they will quickly see at the forefront in reviews that it's a sketchy or dodgy neighbourhood, and your bookings will start to dwindle. How many stores are boarded up in the neighbourhood? Do homes around have pride of ownership, or are there bars on the windows? What is the crime rate like in the area? How are the schools ranked?

"Good" Bones

Does the house have good or bad bones? What's the foundation like? Foundation issues can cost tens of thousands of dollars, and you can quickly get in over your head. Watch for wonky flooring and cracks in the walls—inside and outside. If you think anything seems a little off, have a professional check it out for your peace of mind. It could be that a joist was cut in the basement for a pipe, or a structural post was removed. Or it could be a supporting beam is sitting on sand and sinking. Sometimes it's cheaper to tear down than to renovate. But make sure you know if you're working with a little issue or something to walk away from. Get a professional in!

Never-ending renovations

Some people (myself included) love visualizing and designing and can get excited with all the work they can do. However, the more work you do to a home, the more surprises you'll find out—and the more expenses.

Stay away from projects that include renovations around every room, floor, wall, trim, door, window, etc., unless you have been doing this forever, in which case I don't think you would be reading this book. Or maybe the market research shows a huge gap for growth, and you have a buffer in there for unexpected issues.

Bending over backward

Don't feel you need to suck up to authority or kiss someone's feet. Some cities across the world will pay you to move there and start a business. I'm not saying you should buy and sell properties in these communities, but I want to illustrate that some authorities are much more eager and willing to work with people than others.

Some municipalities make it so hard for you to get a permit for renovations and are stuck in their old-school ways. It can be like pulling teeth to get permission to do the smallest of renovations. Other municipalities, townships, cities, and so forth give grants and promote updating, upgrading, and making homes more energy efficient. If you think it's going to be a headache to do what you need to do to a property in a specific location, I would say pass and save yourself the headache. You have a gut and intuition for a reason—listen to it.

Taj Mahaling the house

This is not an actual term (at least not yet), so don't try to Google it. This is a phrase for what I call *overdoing* a home. It doesn't mean the house is a money pit, but that the buyer has decided to dump too much money into the home for things he or she won't be able to recoup.

Back to the homework and research of a property. If the highest comparable in the area is $700,000, don't put all the bells and whistles in yours, expect to get $1,100,000, and say, "Yeah, but mine has this and this and this, so it's worth $400,000 more."

I'm sorry, my friend, but that means you have *Taj Mahaled* the property, and you might get $780,000 or $850,000 max. Don't overdo it with all the fancy things and think you're going to make it the best of the best. Often, people will just go to another neighbourhood where homes are a million to 1.5 million where they feel the other homes around match the home better; perhaps there are also bigger yards, more square footage, better landscaping, etc. Tread carefully (specifically if you're a shiny object–syndrome buyer)

Insurance Issues

If your insurance company is giving you issues and saying *x* and *x* are voided or exempt from flooding, hurricane, monsoon, and so forth, be leery. I own two homes on floodplains. One flooded two days after I renovated it, and I lost an entire season and probably a year from start to finish. Meanwhile, that road had flooded only one time in the twenty-five years prior. I just happened to get lucky, but it was a risk I was willing to take. When was the last hurricane or earthquake? What exactly is not covered? What is covered? Are you able to get more coverage for a small amount additional every month?

Repeated Sales

How many times has the property changed hands? Were the last two listings designated as "as is" sales or in mid-renovation? Why do people keep buying to renovate it and then giving up? I suggest that you talk to the neighbours. There's always that one neighbour in every subdivision who knows everything about every house and every family and will be happy to share all the details with anyone who will listen.

If you can't find that neighbour. Google the address. You might be able to find police reports that include breaking and entering, or maybe a crime (or multiple crimes) happened in or around the home. Again, it's just a homework thing. I know some of you thought this was going to be easy (and it is!), but you still need to be smart about it as there is work to be done.

So suck it up, buttercup.

Delusional Sellers

I had a seller who wanted to leave each of her three children $125,000, and she also wanted to have money left over for herself. She felt $500,000 would give her a cushion as she planned to rent after selling the house. Now that sounds fine and dandy, right? That amount would give her and her kids what she wanted and what they'd be happy with, end of story, let's sell it. However, the solds in the area of similar age and size were selling for $229,000. Although the house wasn't a money pit, with this seller's mentality, it would become one in this example if you paid her asking price.

Part 3

Designing Your New Investments

> Real estate investing, even on a very small scale,
> remains a tried and true means of building an
> individual's cash flow and wealth
>
> —Robert Kiyosaki

Whether you plan to buy to flip or rent long or short-term, you're going to need to pay attention to design. It can make or break your investment! I enjoy interior design because I love "pretty" things. I also love seeing the change from something so ugly and awful and out-of-date that it makes you wish you had socks, long pants, and a gallon of hand sanitizer, and then you walk into the house three months later and it has become a jaw-dropper. It's kind of like how I always see the best and the potential in people; I also like to see the house in the best version of itself as well. Renovations make this possible for me!

If I have a limited budget, what should I splurge on or put some solid money into?

I am a fan of cheap, but when it comes down to it, I'm smart and middle-of-the-road about it. I can go for high-end if it makes sense for the property. If you plan to sell at a high price point, for example, you're not going to have laminate counters in any of the bathrooms or the kitchen, but in lower price points, that's totally allowable and expected.

It's the same with flooring. You can get away with a better-quality laminate, ceramic floor tile, or vinyl in a cheaper to a mid-price point, but in a higher-end home, they will want the hardwoods and engineered floors. You just have to use your eyes and your brain when evaluating your properties.

Roof

If the shingles are curling up, it doesn't matter how beautiful the kitchen or the master suite is, there is no disguising or photoshopping that roof. (Okay, you can photoshop it, but when they drive up you're busted.) Seeing a roof in a state of disrepair could potentially stop them from even coming inside, and they could instead just back right down the driveway and drive away—I've seen it happen many times. First appearances are key to monetizing your property. It sounds bad, but it's kind of like Tinder. They see that roof and they're swiping left.

Kitchen

Properly renovate the kitchen so that it will show well to potential purchasers or tenants. This doesn't mean you have to break the bank—just complete it. I showed a house recently with lovely flooring, cabinetry, counter, and lighting, and then I got to the tiles and saw they were out of 1962. Why do everything else and leave the dated tiles? Why not fully finish the job/reno? Laziness? Stupidity?

Just sayin'.

There's a saying that has to do with putting a chandelier in a haunted house: it just doesn't go. If you don't want to redo the whole kitchen, at least do what you can to update the appearance. For example, you can change the front cabinet doors. No matter what colour you paint them, dated cabinet doors give away the age.

Make sure you have lots of drawers, as everyone likes drawers. But they won't like cupboards where everything is packed inside and falling over and exploding out of the tight spaces. If it's doable, have the slow-close or soft-close doors and drawers. If soft close is something that people have come to expect in renovated or new kitchens, and it won't break your budget to offer this in your home, bonus.

Countertops and handles are also an easy job, and *please, oh, please,* do not do the countertops yourself. You know those three-step jobbies with the sandy grit and then the shellac type surface on top? *Do not do this.* Hardware stores, please, oh please take these damn products off the shelf!

Please. I am begging you, and I don't beg often.

If you want to do that on your garage floor, knock yourself out, but leave your crafty do-it-yourself counter-type epoxy out of the kitchen.

A word to the wise or from the wise (you know what I mean): when redoing your kitchen, please do NOT use colours in your counters. Avoid like the plague red, purple, blue, green, and I don't care if it's granite—*don't* do it! I have, however, done the odd island in a colour, but not the counter. Just don't!

Your appliances should match. I don't mean that they all have to be the same brand, but depending on how low or high of a price point you're aiming for, they may need to be. In general, the colour should match. You may not have a white fridge, black stove, and stainless dishwasher—not on my watch, sorry. I don't care if you say, "But they all work!" Sorry, I am trumping that.

Unless you're at an incredibly high price point, you don't have to spend a ton of money on appliances. I've seen people spend over $20,000 on appliances in neighbourhoods where they may get $7,500 for their kitchen reno counting the cupboards, so don't be wasteful.

If you're adding a backsplash, please don't go to the clearance section and get your tiles there. I'm not saying I have never bought tiles on sale before, but make sure you know the trending styles, and if they're on sale, then more power to you. But if you don't know the recent trends and happen to pick up tiles for half price that were in style fifteen years ago, someone will have to rip them out, and they won't want the headache. Or if they are okay with the headache, they will take it off the price they want to pay you.

If you're doing a full-kitchen renovation, examine the current layout: Does it make the most sense in its current layout for the profit you're looking to make? How is the flow? Is the kitchen open to other rooms? Are there walls that can come down to make a more fluid and congruent entertaining and cooking space?

Bathroom

Bathroom vanity heights used to be much lower than they are now. If you throw a new counter on an old low vanity, people will know it's an old vanity with a new counter. You can get vanities for cheap, so get a new one, and it will most likely be cheaper in the end anyway. This way potential buyers will know you didn't skip corners and are less likely to lowball you because they know it's quality and not a quick flip. If you can have drawers inside the actual cupboards, then that's good for functionality, and a bonus but not a must-have.

Do not cheap out and get the old low toilets if you're renovating your bathroom. Pay the twenty-dollar extra for the higher one so they won't feel like they're falling on the ground when they sit down. If you redo everything in the bathroom and keep your old toilet, it will stand out like a sore thumb. Speaking of toilets, one of the weirdest things I see quite commonly in bathrooms is massive rooms, but the toilet is so close to the wall your shoulder is touching it. Don't do this!

While some people like the look of a pedestal sink, functionally, they suck. Where do you put anything? The only place I can ever see a pedestal sink (and I still wouldn't do it) would be a powder room. If you're doing an ensuite and can fit a double sink, that's the way to go. If you have to do one sink only, then that's okay, but make sure the height is high, not like the old-fashioned lower ones.

Also, a pretty faucet is so much nicer than the cheapest faucet. I sold a condo recently that had a nice new kitchen faucet, then when I went to the bathroom, voila, there was the old kitchen faucet. Do not put the kitchen faucet in the bathroom or vice versa. Jeepers, people. You don't have to spend $10,000 or more to have the prettiest things, but you can spend $500 more and have beautiful things so your property is not basic. Believe me, your buyers and tenants will notice the difference.

If there's only one bathroom and a second can't be added, do *not* make it just a shower unless you live in an adult living community. People want a bath for bathing children or indulging in their own bubble baths and mini spa escapes. If you're adding a bathroom in the basement, do not make it a two-piece/half bath. People have teenagers who want to live in the basement and have their own shower or guests who will want their own space. Two-piece bathrooms belong on main floors of two-story homes, not in basements with bedrooms, rec rooms, and so forth.

Also, do not spend money on the flooring, the vanity, and the tiles around the tub—then leave an old, low tub. It might cost you $299 to $399 for a new higher back tub with clean modern lines, and I urge you to buy the new one. If the space is large enough to have a separate tub and shower, then do it. Do not have two tubs in the same room. This seems obvious; however, I just sold a home with acreage like that. That's weird, people. What are you cheersing your spouse while you both have a bath for? You are probably in the bath to escape, not to talk with them; if you want to cheers them, buy a hot tub.

If it's a yearly rental, a shower curtain will suffice. But if it's a flip or a nicer short-term rental, then be sure to install a separate shower with glass. Make sure your shower bed is done properly so water doesn't pool and cause issues. Also, make sure there's a fan in the bathroom for humidity, especially if it's a rental, and more showers going on than the norm.

Bathrooms are certainly key spaces to focus on when renovating, but be smart about it. I went to a bathroom place about ninety minutes from my home because I was told by a contractor to go pick my vanities, toilets, and hardware and to give myself two hours to pick everything for a new build I was doing. He set up an appointment for me, and I made my trek down. I was there for maybe twenty minutes max and apologized for wasting the woman's time, but I said I wouldn't be buying anything.

There were less than ten vanities, priced $3,500 and up. The cheapest toilet was $900, and the tap and faucet selection were also minuscule and overpriced. I don't have a problem paying $3,500 or more for a vanity if it's unique and in a high-end home, but when it looks like the ones for which I pay $799, I'm not bending over and taking it (pardon the visual).

It's the same with the toilets. They were as nice as a "shitter" could be, but I don't need toilets that open on their own (that cost even more) and the ones that didn't do any fancy things or have a built-in bidet that looked exactly the same as the ones I could buy at a home hardware store for under $329.

Lighting

I don't know why people do half-ass renovations and don't complete them. If you're redoing your tiles, vanity, and tub, then redo your lighting too. Don't keep all the huge light bulbs that will make your buyers feel like they're a beauty pageant kid backstage. Update the lighting—and mirrors, if need be.

Be sure to make the lighting bright enough in the bathroom. One, for functionality for women to apply makeup; two, for men to pluck those pesky nose hairs. Also, consider the positioning of the light. A light over a stand-alone tub can really be a focal point in an ensuite (lovely window and scenery behind if you want bonus points). Do your best to have good natural light. If you have some privacy, a huge window by a stand-alone tub is lovely. If privacy is not an option, then a horizontal slim window up at a higher level is nice for extra light and visual appeal.

Flooring

Tiles are so inexpensive and look so much better than linoleum flooring. (Please, can we get rid of the linoleum! Stop selling it in stores—we can only pray.) There are tons of laminate floors that cost less than two dollars a square foot. You don't need eight-dollar-per-foot flooring. Now if you're in an estate subdivision and doing a custom home, they might insist on engineered hardwood, but for a typical flip, fixer-upper or rental, that extra spend is unnecessary.

Other parts of the house

Lighting

Don't underestimate the importance of lighting throughout the home. All the lighting fixtures should be updated, and *please* stay in the same theme or genre. Don't put a brand-new Victorian- style light in the dining room and then a modern light in the bedroom. If you're unsure about light styles, go into a light store. Tell them how many bedrooms you have, how many fixtures are in common areas such as the kitchen, dining room, and living room so they won't let you be a mismatched, hot mess.

Do not buy the boob lights (you know, the ones with the half circles with the thing/nipple in the middle). Worse are the flycatchers, as I call them, from the '70s or '80s—why they still sell them, I will never know. They're the ones that are kind of like between a plate and a bowl, and all the dead flies seem to accumulate there. I'm not saying you should break the bank, but depending on the age of the home, you will need to update the lighting for sure.

Front door

If the front door is dated, fix it, paint it, or replace it. If it has an old, floral-type glass, change out the insert for something more modern. You don't have to change the whole door, just the glass. Doors are expensive. Door handles are also an easy and stylish way to update a home on the interior doors (watch for sales or price matching).

Fireplace

If there's a fireplace, update it with tiles, stonework, or paint. Paint out the brass for black, and you could even paint any existing front floor tiles to a more neutral colour like gray, black, or white. The funkier colours that may be there depending on the age of the home and fireplace will date the home. Also, make sure the vent covers don't look ratty or rusty and that they are all the same style and colour.

You've seen a house where it looks like a few chair legs have gone through the vent cover in the dining room, or they're rusty and covered in hair and dust. Yuck, please change these to have more fluidity in the home. They're one of many things, like the finishing touches and icing on top of the cake that could make or break your sale.

Light switches

Make sure all the light switches are the same style and colour. Sometimes you'll see a home with yellow light switch covers but with white switches or vice versa, or sometimes they will be broken or ill-fitting. These are super cheap to replace so make sure they are all consistent. Small details like this go a long way toward your overall visual appeal.

Accent walls

I'm a fan of accent walls, perhaps because I get bored easily. I don't mean three walls of grey and one of green; I mean a wall of brick, shiplap, or barn board, for example. Sometimes, I make an accent wall in a living room, and sometimes I make one in the bedroom as a headboard wall. You don't need to limit yourself to the dining room or living room here—change it up. I feel it adds some depth and makes it a bit different, especially if the neighbours all have cookie-cutter homes with the same layout. I've even done a steel headboard wall. It sounds odd, I know, but it looked amazing with rope lights with Edison bulbs and knots hanging on either side of the king-size bed. That was a fun condo flip I did—it made that unit stand out over the hundreds of identical units in those complexes, and I sold it for the highest price any of those units had ever gone for.

Ceiling

Shave the popcorn ceiling off (the little bumpies up there that date the home), and change it to a flat ceiling. And worse than the popcorn is the swooshes done by hand back in the day. You must get rid of these swooshes, or you will be screaming the age of the home and the last renovation date.

If you can vault a ceiling, you should do so. Depending on your budget, the comparables in the neighbourhood, and of course, the rafters, there's often an easy way to vault a ceiling. Where I am currently sitting has an eighteen-foot ceiling. The room isn't very large, but it doesn't feel small due to the height of the ceiling. When I purchased this home, it had a flat roof (not ideal for Canadian winters and snow), which was leaking, and I knew it wouldn't make it through another winter.

Because it had low seven-foot ceilings, and I already knew the roof needed to be done and vaulted, I inquired with the fellow doing the framing. I said, "I'm no engineer, and this might not be doable, but how much would it be to vault this ceiling to eighteen feet?" I'd picked eighteen feet as a random number as I had a condo conversion loft in Toronto at that time with an eighteen-foot ceiling, which was my favourite.

The one trussing and roof quote to change it to a non-flat roof and make it a typical eight-foot ceiling was $21,000 and change, while the other quote for an eighteen-foot ceiling was $22,000 and change. I was shocked, but that was a no-brainer; I'd pay $1,000 and a bit all day long, and I would have paid more, to be honest. It was totally worth it! Amen! Thank you, Ceiling Gods and Goddesses!

Painting

The paint should be fresh with no borders or wallpaper unless it's been trendy in the last year (and that would be wallpaper only as I haven't seen a trendy border in forever). Painting a little can go a long way. You'd be surprised by how many people looking at your place won't want to paint. They'll see an awful colour and think, "Oh, that will probably take five coats to cover!" Then they'll overanalyze how much "work" the home needs and pass on it.

You want potential buyers or renters to say, "Wow this room is a great size, I love the natural light and the beautiful floors, and just look at those high baseboards."

If they see a dated paint job, they'll see only the problem. This is also common in life, as people see the problem, hurdle, or roadblock, but not the outcome and what's on the other side should a certain action be taken. So show your potential buyers the bigger picture and the best version of your house by doing the painting upfront so they don't have to imagine it for themselves.

Spaces

How many bedrooms are in the home? Are there any other spaces that could be used or converted to a higher and better-serving use? Sometimes you'll have an attic space that could be finished or an oversized storage room that could be a bonus bedroom, kid's play area, music room, or office.

Maximizing the home's usable space adds value. If a renovation is in the budget, and it makes sense, then all the power to you, but if it's not there, think outside the box. Perhaps there's a room not fully finished or an unfinished, oversized furnace room, and part of that space can be stolen from to make better use and maximize the home's square footage.

Look for the opportunities, and conquer and eliminate the annoyances in the home. A simple example is the lack of a front hall closet in a home. Many people will not notice if a home has no front closet, especially if the coatrack has been removed in home staging until they try to put their coat away and realize the closet is twenty feet from the front door. How annoying and nonfunctional that would be! Depending on the width of the hallway, maybe a closet can be added. Or maybe the garage is right next to the house's entrance and space can be bumped into the garage to make this new front hall closet while still allowing enough room in the garage to park a vehicle.

See how you can make the space better and more optimal. For example, I bought a home with no interior garage entrance (actually, I have bought a few). The home was situated so that you walked in and directly in front of you was the powder room. Down the hall to the left was the main living space, and directly to the right was a wall, and behind it, the garage. I blew a hole through into the garage, added steps, and for around $1,000, I had an inside garage entrance.

People also love an income suite. Maybe you can add a granny or nanny suite above your garage. Or maybe your basement is unfinished, and you use it for junk storage and let the kids draw on the floor with chalk. You could turn it into a basement apartment. Finding ways for yourself or others to make money month over month is never a bad idea.

However, if you're in a higher-end area, I would make a bar in the basement, such as an entertainment and lounge space for parties with a wet bar, wine fridge, and perhaps a wine cellar. People purchasing at this price point neither think of renters and tenants nor show their neighbours that they need that income to support living in that neighbourhood.

Is there any space that you could turn into either year-round living or partial-year living? For example, at a home I purchased, there was a lean-to that they used for wood storage as it had a woodstove. I turned that into a bedroom and closed it in. Or perhaps you could turn a deck with overhang into a year-round sunroom or bonus living room. There are always things you can do you just need to look for them and be creative.

Front yard

How is the parking situation? Is it a single-lane driveway? How big is the front yard? Could you steal some grass space to create double-wide parking? Does it have the old patio steps up to the front door that are probably original to the builder? What more aesthetically- and pocket-pleasing alternatives can you create? Do the lights outside look like they are original to the house with different-coloured light bulbs that you did one Christmas and never changed? Are they tarnished because they've seen better days? Could they use some paint or do you just need all new exterior fixtures?

Unfortunately, you will have to look at the "unpretty things" as people can be fooled temporarily by pretty kitchens and bathrooms. But they will look at the age and condition of the windows, roof, and furnace or heating source. Make sure all these items are up to par so people don't go subtracting ludicrous amounts from your asking price. Because that's what they'll do. They'll guesstimate what they think it will cost to redo or change, even if you have already taken these lack of upgrades into consideration with the pricing. So save both of you the trouble, and update what you can up front.

Flooring

Make sure there's no weird gapping on the floor, such as what happens when some people put laminate in but didn't let it sit in the house for three days to acclimatize to the space and temperature.

Also, make sure all the transition strips are down where one type of flooring transitions to the next. I've mentioned that I don't like linoleum, but I must ask that you try not to mismatch flooring. There's nothing worse than going into a home with hardwood in the dining room, blue carpet in the living room, laminate in the hallway, another laminate in one bedroom, beige carpet in one bedroom, and light fuchsia carpet in the other bedroom. The hair is standing up on my neck even as I write this, and my body is cringing at the thought.

Try to have one floor throughout the home—or two at the maximum. Maybe you have hardwood or laminate everywhere except the carpet in the kids' bedrooms or the basement, which could be vinyl in case it floods. Just try to keep flooring differences to a minimum—pretty please!—with whip cream and a cherry on top. PS: I'm not counting bathrooms. You don't need to have the same flooring in the living room, master bathroom, kids' bathroom, and so forth.

Closets

I'm a sucker for large closets. If there's any way you can increase the size of a closet, do it! You can steal from another room or closet, from a hallway—depending on how it's configured—or a mudroom, sunroom, or garage. It's always nice to have a large closet. I've never seen someone walk into a closet and say, "No, no, this is too big. This is a waste of space!" That just doesn't happen. When clients walk into large closets, they will hear angel music and harps strumming as a soft light beams down from above.

Curb appeal

Pay attention to the curb appeal of your house, as that may be the deciding factor whether the buyers or renters even walk through the front door. Do they pull up and see a dinged-up garage that looks like a team of hockey players have used it as their goalie net for twenty years? Or is the wood rotted and you can pull the splinters apart with your fingertips? If this sounds like your house, then a new garage door is on your checklist.

The same goes for siding or brick. Has someone barbecued too close and warped the siding or backed a car into the corner and dented it? If so, this needs to be fixed or replaced. Is the brickwork anywhere (oftentimes below windows) crumbling and breaking? If so, this needs to be repaired as you don't want to deter buyers and send them to newer builds thinking yours is a problem or a money pit house only disguised with a pretty kitchen and bathroom. There are some nice stone veneers out there that could be a possibility for your home, but make sure you research your prices.

Can you add any landscaping or even architectural design if the home is somewhat flat and boring? A few items to consider include laying down fresh sod and having the driveway freshly coated. This adds to your curb appeal and makes your house pristine and welcoming to prospective buyers and renters, as well as demonstrating pride of ownership.

Maybe the home can't be seen from the road because the plants, trees, and bushes are so overgrown? Or maybe it has a beautiful view of rolling hills blocked by a large cedar hedge? I bought a waterfront home once, but there were so many trees and bushes and overgrown brush between the home and the waterfront it looked like it backed onto a forest. I kept four large, beautiful trees along the shoreline and had the rest cleared for a beautiful view of windsurfers, kayakers, boaters, canoe enthusiasts, stand-up paddle boarders, wildlife, and sensational sunsets.

What are some no-no design investments?

While you will have many choices about what types of renovations you should do, there are also many renovations you should *not* do. Unfortunately, there isn't a one-size-fits-all answer as every property is unique, and so many variables come into play. Make sure you've done your research, know what price point you should be selling in, and what those other homes have.

Although I've said it before and will say it again that real estate investing is easy, this does not mean it comes without homework and research. I'd have to say that is the most important part of the real estate investing game. Know your neighbourhood, and don't compare to locations that don't apply to you. See apples for apples and oranges for oranges.

Basement

What does your basement currently look like? Maybe a basement apartment doesn't work in the price point you're in. Maybe you need a wet bar, a movie room, an extra bedroom and bathroom, or a wine cellar. You need to know your market and appeal to the kinds of buyers who will be considering your property. Maybe it's a popular hunting area, and you need a designated gun room.

I don't advise against moving things to the basement that are functional where they are. For example, spending the cash to move a laundry room from upstairs to the basement is not going to get you more money and will hurt you. Save that money for renovations that make sense to most—if not all—of your potential buyers.

Eliminating bedrooms

Don't eliminate two main-floor bedrooms of a bungalow to make a big walk-in closet and master suite. Yes, I'm sure that will be lovely, but how functional is it for someone to have a one-bedroom house? What if they have kids? What if they have guests over? What if they need an office? Most buyers will want the flexibility of the space over anything else.

Extra insulation

Don't waste time and money by adding extra insulation in the walls. People are not going to see this, and unless it's too cold or you're going to be living there and want cheaper utility bills, no one's going to know or see the benefit or want to pay you more for it. Only renovate what they can see (besides structural things that have to be done, foundations, roof, etc.).

Not enough doors

What kind of outdoor space do you have? People will want to get to the backyard from inside the house. They won't want to go out the front door and walk all the way around the house to get to the backyard. If there's no interior door to the backyard, add one so people can easily go outside to enjoy the space to entertain, have a barbeque, and so forth.

Proper window repairs

I'm a fan of natural light, but what if the home has tons of huge windows, from floor to ceiling, but they're old, the seals are gone, and the glass is foggy? You could replace them, but this is super costly. Alternatively, you could have the argon removed. This is done through a little hole about the size of a pinky fingernail. Or you could replace the glass if the moldings and trim are still good and have not rotted.

What do buyers typically not want?

Some renovations may seem like a good idea to you, but it may be good for you—and you alone. Over the years, I've developed a pretty solid list of what I see buyers tend to pass on when viewing a property. If you already have these elements listed below, you'll have to make do, but please don't add them in thinking they will garner more money for your sale.

Solar panels

Despite global warming, trying to sell a home with solar panels is a pain in the butt. Most buyers don't see the value, and if they do see them as beneficial, they may not understand the cost to have solar panels installed and won't want to pay to what you did in return. Another big issue with solar panels is that when the roof needs to be replaced, there will be an added cost of removing them and having them reinstalled.

Rented equipment

People also don't want to take on the cost of rented furnaces or air-conditioning units. If you need a new unit, put it on your visa and pay it off. Then your buyers won't be stuck with a contract and a massive buyout.

Overly renovated

Be cautious of your neighbourhood when considering increasing the size of your home. If you're on a tiny lot and can't do any addition, don't dump loads of money into your home. You may have put the nicest counter and nicest bathroom to flip a big profit. But if someone would rather live farther from a particular eyesore of an area, have an extra eight hundred square feet, or be closer to that park, then you are screwing yourself and wasting money where it's not needed.

Outdoor extras

Try to stay away from specific outdoor extras. I had a client who put in a basketball court, tennis court, mini golf range, and mini putt outside. This is great and dandy and fun if you enjoy these activities, but he will not be recouping the hundreds of thousands of dollars he spent on these features.

Quirky and weird

Although I'm a lover of tiles and unique pieces, quirky can become weird for buyers, and you can pigeonhole yourself in a potential sale. It's okay to step outside of the box the odd time and maybe in smaller spaces such as a shower niche.

For example, try not to put bright red tile in a kitchen; unless you're short-term renting it and want a funky, different space for people to visit, then I would make an exception. Otherwise, a buyer is going to be staring at it for a month and shaking their heads wondering why the previous owner picked such a specific and not timeless tile. Take into account whether you plan to flip or hold it for twenty years when considering quirky.

It's generally not a good idea to make a space too unique to you. I have a contractor who had a client who visited Peru and had a breakthrough in his life while at a church. He asked the church if he could purchase the particular pew he was sitting on when he had this visualization that day, and they agreed to let him do so.

He then spent over $100,000 renovating a bathroom at his home by replicating the church and designing it into this bathroom (for what reason, I will never know). As you can guess, 99.9 percent of buyers that come into this bathroom are going to think it's odd and would not want to give him the money that he paid for the whole project; they'll be also calculating how much it would cost to switch it back to "typical" and "normal." This is an extreme example of why you should never over-customize a home, room, or project.

Also, do not go over the top with landscaping. Simple landscaping is fine, but over-the-top landscaping, with designers and so forth, won't ever return to your pocket. If you want to live in that home, and that's your enjoyment, then knock yourself out. But if you think spending that money will be returned to you when you sell it, keep dreaming. Moderation, my friends, moderation.

Wallpaper

To be honest, I have never wallpapered anywhere. I'm not saying I haven't liked places with wallpaper; however, styles change so quickly so I don't like to limit myself. It's such a pain to remove so I just skip it.

I sold a house where the owner, a wallpaper salesman, had retired fifteen years before and had done every square inch including inside the closets (shoot me now) in the most popular, expensive wallpaper available at the time. He said, "I spent over $150,000 on wallpaper in this house." If that is true, then he should never be given any money to do design ever again.

But even if it's factual, a current buyer is only going to see headaches and nightmares at the thought of all that wallpaper. They will probably want $10,000 off the asking price for the sheer annoyance as they will have to repair the walls after the wallpaper is removed and repaint the entire home.

Looking ahead

You need to know your market and selling price. You may be in the price range where people will want all the bells and whistles, so don't discount anything before researching the competition and who you're up against and what they have in their homes. When spending, know your numbers so you don't get ripped off and spend more money where you don't need to and won't get that extra return and then some back.

As your investments pay off, you'll likely end up buying bigger projects. Originally, you might be happy to net $35,000 after everything is finished. Then you're working in the $150,000 range, then in the half-million to a three-quarter range. Soon you won't do a deal that won't make you at least two million dollars; it can easily be a climbing scale.

You'll buy in nicer neighbourhoods. You'll spend $200,000 on interiors, not counting the house purchase. Everything will be the exact same but on a larger scale. You'll have more skin in the game, and the risk is higher, but the profits are also that much higher. I know some people who don't like to have all their eggs in one basket (or one house or job), and that's fine as you should always invest at your comfort level. If $500,000 or less in purchase price of homes is your niche, then there's nothing wrong with that.

Maybe as your bank account grows, you want to venture into other projects. Maybe you want to buy an old factory and turn it into condominiums or purchase a church and turn it into a nightclub or a bed and breakfast. It's all the same, but on a bigger scale and more fun if you ask me. But hey, we're all different.

When you have more money and experience, you aren't in the same pool with other first-time buyers and investors. There's less chance of a bidding war and a better chance that you can get a much more significant amount off the asking price because the pool of buyers is drastically smaller.

Part 4

What to Do with Your Real Estate

Real estate cannot be lost or stolen, nor can it be carried
away. Purchased with common sense, paid for in full, and
managed with reasonable care, it is about the safest
investment in the world.

—Franklin D. Roosevelt

Currently, I'm switching all my properties from long-term
rentals to short-term rentals or selling them if they don't
conform. I've discovered that I make more in a week renting
short-term than I do in a month long-term; however, some
places are simply not conducive to becoming short-term
rentals. Who knows—maybe in the future I will switch them
back to yearly rentals as markets and renters change.

**How do I decide whether to use my real estate for
long-term leases or short-term rentals?**

This analysis should ideally be done before a property is
purchased, but as in my case above, situations may change. For
the short-term rentals on sites such as Airbnb, you need to
determine who would be your ideal renter. Where would they
be living? What would their budget be? Would they drive to
where your property is located?

Check out your short-term rental competition, and do your
homework to consider how your rental compares to the others

around you. What are the other hosts in your area charging? Were you hoping for $299 a night, and they're only charging $85? How often are they booked? What do their reviews say? Does your unit have anything the others don't? If not, how can you make yours more desirable? Maybe you have a cool gaming area or mural wall. Perhaps you have a hanging hammock in the living room or a really unique décor.

(Side note, I definitely recommend professional photos!)

If a short-term rental doesn't seem feasible, what have prices been for monthly rentals in the area? After analyzing the numbers, would it still make sense for you to purchase the property? You don't want to buy a property and realize that neither short nor long-term work out financially for you. Gulp!

Let's look at a couple of things to consider when weighing the option of short term versus long term rentals.

Ideal for short-term rentals

- ❑ in the city centre
- ❑ near nightlife/sports domes/concerts/major attractions
- ❑ funky space
- ❑ walking distance to many things (if in the city centre; if it is waterfront, this doesn't apply)
- ❑ space for tons of beds and pullout couches
- ❑ waterfront

- ❑ near skiing
- ❑ near casino

Ideal for long-term rentals

- ❑ typical subdivision (unless you have a pool or something that most people don't have at home)
- ❑ nothing special about it, builder grade
- ❑ two-unit home such as duplex
- ❑ lots of parking

How do I design a short-term rental?

If you choose to short-term monetize your rental, think about fun and comfort. I recommend that you create Instagram-worthy areas that are colourful and grab the guests' attention. People like to flaunt their lives, where they are, what they're doing, and where they're staying. My units are stylish and well-decorated from an interior decorator perspective. I include spots for Instagram or TikTok such as a graffiti wall, a swing, a hammock over the water, a neon light that says something cheeky, and so forth—spots where they can show off and post everything about their getaway. The more spots you have, the better, as renters will change outfits and pretend the photos or videos are taken on different days. I'm sure some of you are rolling your eyes, but that's the current reality of how some people function.

If your unit looks like every other cookie-cutter unit, it will get rented, sure, but will it be all the time when there isn't a concert in town or during a global pandemic? Absolutely not—you need to stand out. My properties were busier during the COVID-19 pandemic than they were before because everyone was so bored trapped at home and craved something different. They wanted the fun uniqueness of my spaces. Make yours stand out. For example, in Croatia, my friend stayed at a place that looked like the Batcave, and it even had a creepy Joker behind a blind curtain area. That is not my style; however, it is unique and different. How will yours stand out?

My cluster on the waterfront that I am currently developing will have aspects of Bali so that Torontonians can drive ninety minutes instead of approximately twenty-two hours in flight to get a similar effect. (Well, obviously, not the whole island but at the very least some cool pics.)

In short, inspire your guests to take photos and videos in every inch of your space. Make them want to make their friends jealous. (Have you ever had a friend go away, and they usually post about everything, food, and so forth, and then they're gone away, and it's crickets? They're staying somewhere un-Instagrammable, guaranteed.)

Now obviously, these are first-world problems when people are concerned about what other people are thinking about them, but if your place is pretty, unusual, hip, funky, different, or unique, it will be rented more often. Then other people will ask them where that shot was taken and will want to stay there. It snowballs, and then as the host/owner, you keep upping and upping your prices (cha-ching!).

Also, create lots of places for people to sleep. For example, I have two one-bedroom cottages, and both sleep eight people. It sounds odd for a one-bedroom, but they both have a bed, a pullout couch, and a bunkie with two beds. The more you can sleep, then the guests can divide the cost between them and the higher your occupancy will be and the more you can charge.

You will also need basic supplies, such as plates, cups, linens, shampoo, and conditioner. Don't go over the top with high-end plates or anything like that, as some will go missing, and some will get smashed. Make sure your cupboards aren't bare or stocked with Styrofoam or paper plates.

Also, make sure you give lots of pointers. This can be as easy as looking up on Google, like things to do in your town or city, and copying and pasting it to a saved tab on whatever platform you are renting through. Do this same thing for best spots to eat, bus schedules, how to get to the airport, and so forth. You only need to do it once, and people will think you're so thoughtful and thorough and are more likely to leave you a glowing review.

How do I decide whether to keep or flip my real estate investment?

When purchasing real estate, you already know you have several choices to monetize your property. You can flip it immediately (after renovations, that is) or keep it. If you're holding onto your property, you can live in it and allow the value to grow or rent it out to others on a short or long-term basis. Do your research, crunch your numbers, and see what's most viable for your location and market.

Everyone will have different ideas of what's worth it for them. I wouldn't flip a house for $10,000, $20,000, or even $40,000; however, many people would, especially in the beginning. Real estate investing is on a ladder/scale, and you have to start somewhere. To get the higher returns, you require a higher budget to buy and renovate, and that doesn't come out of thin air; you have to build up to it. Just because I wouldn't flip for those above amounts doesn't mean I didn't do so at one point.

It's best to determine if you are holding or flipping *before* you purchase the property. If you can make a lot of money by flipping, I'd still advise you to consider the long-term outlook. For example, what could you make if you held onto it for another five, ten, or fifteen years? If it's hot now, how hot could it be in a decade? Alternatively, what could you invest in with that cash if you did jump ship right away? Which scenario has a better chance of return?

Sometimes you know you're going to flip right from the beginning. For example, last year, I bought a condo from a client because we have a Your Home Sold Guaranteed program. I'm not the biggest fan of condos for multiple reasons. One is since I like to do additions, that isn't possible, so I'm quite limited. Two, I'm a bit of a control freak. I don't like that the halls could be changed or the floors redone in the common areas, the elevators changed to some tacky design, and the pool, hot tub, and amenity rooms altered all to a style I may be outvoted on. I also don't like paying fees into a reserve fund where someone who is not me makes financial decisions. Also being a dog lover, and a big dog lover specifically, most condos have pet size restraints.

So I knew right away that condo would be a flip. I ripped out the kitchen and bathroom, put in all new flooring and trim, put a brick wall in the kitchen, new lighting fixtures, and Bob's your uncle. I bought it for $195,000 (as she still paid the commission) and sold it for $265,000, having spent only $16,200 on renovations. Not bad for five weeks' work of picking a vanity, kitchen, laminate, and doing a flip I wasn't even planning on.

Sometimes you sell when the property just doesn't work. Say a tenant is annoying me, and I have had annoying tenant after annoying tenant in that space. Two certain homes come to mind where I always had bad luck with tenants. It didn't matter if I renovated, changed bedroom sizes, bathrooms, added decks, fences, etc., they always ended up with crappy renters. I assumed the house (or neighbourhood) was jinxed and dumped them.

Sometimes you sell to get the money out for another project. I currently have three properties for sale as I have a massive waterfront project going on, and I want more of a cushion for the building period (even though the houses I'm selling have great cash flow). I wouldn't have sold them for just any old reason, but it makes sense to do so right now. Utilizing the profits to cushion the project that will cash flow more money is a wise idea.

When you sell a property, you're tapping into a valuable asset to fund something else, but the wisdom in doing so depends on what your goals are. Selling a property can help build that portfolio, and your goals will determine the right time for you to sell. What's important to each person is different, whether that be another real estate investment or to fund their dreams outside of the real estate world. Make sure you have thoroughly reviewed all the pros and cons of selling your properties to ensure it's what you want to do before you sign those documents.

Specifically, I recommend that you investigate the following conditions and scenarios.

The market

Investigate what the market's doing in your region. If the numbers are negligible and not very impressive, keeping a property makes more sense so you can build equity and eventually make another purchase. If you took the profit out of the sold property, what would you use it for? There's no point in taking it out if it will just sit in your account and or be wasted on piddly things and not reinvested in the market.

If you're looking at purchasing a home for $300,000, and you have $100,000 to spend on renovations, and the comparables show $400,000—well, big whoop dee do!—all you will do is recoup your money. But if there's significant value to be gained, now you have something to think about. If the bank gives you $100,000, or you have it, but if the other end shows you'll sell at $400,000, why are you even buying it? There are almost always hidden surprises when it comes to renovations, so that leaves no room for any growth—and most likely loss.

My recommendations keep circling back to the same thing, which is to do your research and check out the comparables to see if you can make money. If you can make money on a $100,000 house, then do it, but if you can't make money on a $525,000 house, don't buy it. Just because the purchase price is higher and you are approved for it doesn't automatically mean that the house will make more money for you in flipping it or as an investment. If you can make money on a million-dollar home, then buy it if the numbers make sense. Have I mentioned that you need to know your numbers? I know I sound like a broken record, but I'm trying to engrave it into your brain.

If the market is stable but not on the rise, I would flip it in case the value doesn't rise regardless if you hold it for one year, five years, or ten years. Is it a buyer's market, a seller's market, or a stable market? See what's currently on the market, how long the listings have been sitting, what's been selling, and how they compare to yours. The last thing you want to do is list your place for four months when you haven't put tenants in because you wanted the place to show well and then get no offers. You will have lost valuable rent during those months.

The neighborhood

When deciding whether to keep a property, of course, you will look at the home, but your determination should also include evaluating if the neighborhood is going up or down. You don't want to hold onto a house just because it's appealing to the eye if the neighbourhood is not ideal. Is the neighbourhood on an incline, flatline, or decline?

If you see trends of a good return, keep your property and refinance. If the area is in growth, see what your banking institution will offer you to refinance. Keep 25 percent or 20 percent or so of the profit in the home/mortgage and remove the rest to reinvest elsewhere.

Usually, you can't refinance for the first year, which limits future projects and the whole ball-rolling aspect. Maybe you have to keep the loan to value at 65/35, and if you have to keep it to 35 percent, that doesn't give you much extra to pull out. Maybe they will keep it at 85/15, and perhaps that gives you enough worth to work with for another project. Even if you pull out enough money, you have to see if a bank will provide you with another mortgage. Just because you have the down-payment money doesn't mean they will lend you the remaining funds needed.

Check with your local city or township as they often have ten, twenty, and even thirty-year plans. They might tell you that a rec centre is going in near your home in seven years. Or maybe they're putting five million dollars toward revitalizing a specific area near your property or making a large park with a splash pad or something fun for the neighborhood kids.

The versatility of the property

Think of your urgency for money: do you need the money now to do another project? How much will that project return to you? What has been the average increase of home value year over year in the area you are considering purchasing in?

For example, could you keep it and use the home for a short-term rental? If your city or town bans short-term rentals, could you rent regularly to tenants? Could you divide it into two units or add another one? What could you do to up the value of the house? How flexible is the space to be used in a multitude of functions? Although I'm not a pessimist as an investor, you have to be smart and think from all angles to cover your bases.

Your tax situation

How many flips have you done this year? Check with your accountant to see if you should sell next year instead. Maybe the money from this flip will put you in a different tax bracket that will make your payout for capital gains higher, which is not ideal.

Politics

Consider the timing for the next big election. Often there's a lull in real estate as people worry about who will get in office and what might change. You don't want to be sitting with a vacant house and paying for staging when no one is looking at your listing.

Stranger things

Always consider the worst of the worst. I bought a property once, and there was a map on the building, and the registry system showed a line right through the house, so it looked like one half was on the property I was purchasing, and the other half was not. It was waterfront property, and the water had gone down over the decades. All the surveys were old, so they were not very accurate.

I had to evaluate if it made sense to buy it if I had to tear that home down and move it. Turns out, I didn't have to tear it down, but even if I had to, the comparables showed it was still a good buy. I have never bought something just to quickly flip to a developer. I'm too home-greedy and I love designing, so I'd rather just keep it and do it myself.

Renovation

If you've done quick cosmetic upgrades to the home but have not improved the quality, I would flip it. Because if you rent it and get renters who "live well" (i.e., rough) in the house, are you going to have to redo everything you just did? If so, then it doesn't make sense to keep it.

Look at how much money you're putting in for renovations. Are you doing the kitchen, knocking out walls, redoing floors, adding a bathroom, updating something on the outside, adding a fence and deck and maybe even a garage? How much are you spending, and how much is it worth at the end?

Big-ticket items

Look at the big-ticket items about the home, and think of how many years will pass before they need to be replaced. Some things may look great now, but how will they look in twelve years? For example, how old is the roof? How old are the windows? What about the furnace or boiler system? Are there municipal sewers? If not, then how old is the septic system? You don't want to be smacked with a $5,000 bill—or possibly even triple that amount—depending on what needs to be replaced in a few years. What if you don't have the money set aside for those repairs and/or replacements, and you didn't consider them when purchasing the property?

Your personal goals and dreams

Have you made your money and now want to use that money for your kids' postsecondary education? Do you want to get your equity out fully or split it in half and buy two investment properties? Do you want to take a year off and travel the world with the money?

Should I try to sell a house when I have tenants in that property?

Yes, absolutely!

While some tenants try their hardest to make it difficult, there are ways around them in most cases. That being said, there are some disgruntled tenants, and depending on how vulgar they are, you may not want to show the property until they're out. But generally, if you're selling a multiplex unit with vacant apartments, that would look incredibly suspicious. Plus, you'd be trying to sell your buyers on potential rather than fact. When your units are tenanted, it shows the cash flow, and the investors can learn your numbers and see if it works for their portfolio. Plus, it's easier to get funding from the bank when there are already concrete leases in place.

If your place is vacant, and you say it "could" and "should" rent for a certain amount, it's hard to run numbers if your buyers don't really know what they can get for it and are unfamiliar with the area or market rents. Also, what if you find tenants but they don't want to move in for two to three months, and you're left holding the bill? Seeing tenants in a property is key to showing that it's a desirable place to live. Even if I was looking for something for me, and the people were a little rough but not super rough, I would think of them as a "renter for life" as opposed to the cluttered, dirty, or unmaintained apartment they may be living in.

I've shown homes where tenants have lived for sixteen, nineteen, and even thirty-seven years! The fellow that lived in the unit for thirty-seven years was one in a fourplex on a rougher street, but it had a liquor store, movie theatre, restaurants and nightclubs within walking distance. The amount of money that fellow has spent on a property that he will never own baffles my mind, but hey, he pays his rent every month.

How do I inform tenants that I'm going to sell the property?

If I'm the owner and I want to sell, I can't simply tell the tenants that I'm selling and that they have to move: I must have an accepted agreement of purchase and sale, then I can give them proper notice and serve the proper forms. Even then, I can't ask them to move just because I sold the property. An acceptable reason would be that the new owner, the spouse of the new owner, the new owner's parents, the spouse's parents, their child, or their spouse's child plans to move in. If they're month-to-month renters, then immediately, they have sixty days from when I give them written notice.

If it's a yearly lease, then I would have to wait until their lease is over unless the tenant agrees to terminate the lease early. Some tenants will leave for free, and some will need to be bought out. A common buyout scenario is that the owner pays first and last month's rent for the tenant elsewhere. In Canada, the form that needs to be signed in relation to this is called an N11. If there's an accepted agreement of purchase and sale, you have to serve what's called in Canada an N12, which indicates who is moving into the property.

Besides getting the tenants out upon mutual agreement and serving the proper forms, you can get them out for other reasons, which include not paying rent, interfering with other tenants in the building, overcrowding, or if you are doing major extensive renovations or tearing the building down. I've never had tenants stay when they're not supposed to do so. However, in Canada, we can call the sheriff to remove them. They don't get a free pass forever; however, sometimes it feels like they do.

Should I engage a realtor to help me sell a property?

Absolutely! (And no, it's not because I'm biased, but because a realtor's knowledge and assistance is essential!)

I tried to sell a property before I was licensed as that was when I wanted to travel the world for three years. I listed it with an agent but then found out that the bank would let me keep it, so I withdrew the listing. I hadn't thought the bank would let me rent it out because, on paper, I was making peanuts. Also, I had another house I lived in, plus a rental, and I hadn't yet built a rapport with the lending institutions as it was early on in my investing career.

I would definitely recommend a realtor, but I advise that you be very careful to choose the right one. Yes, a realtor costs commission, but they protect your interest, and a good one will do their very best job via marketing and their sphere to get you top dollar. So although realtors cost money, it comes out in the wash because they're able to market to more people and get more eyes on the property, which means more money in your pocket in the end when they sell for a higher sales amount by exposing it to tens of thousands of realtors.

Of course, you can't change the location of your home and put it in downtown NYC or London, but realtors can control your property's exposure, which translates to moola for you and your end game. You're responsible for the home's condition and deciding on its final listing price. However, your agent will show you the active listings and solds and do all the comparison numbers to determine the best route in your selling strategy

What's important when it comes to staging a home for prospective buyers?

Make sure your property shows in the best light so you can help your realtor put the best foot forward for potential buyers. Some realtors will offer complimentary staging—but they won't declutter your Tupperware cupboard, which may be is an avalanche of mismatched yogurt containers, never seeming to be two true matches.

Declutter

Speaking of decluttering, when selling a home, you should not have clutter, especially if the space is small. It needs to feel homey and welcoming, emphasizing the areas for kids to play or parents to unwind. You need people to be able to easily picture themselves living there. Make it neutral with odd pops of spunk or colour so it's not blah and institutional-like inside.

Don't bring attention to downfalls in the home in general, but let's look at the kitchen. For example, if there isn't enough storage space, don't throw in an extra piece of furniture exploding with toasters, coffee makers, extra pots and pans, and a microwave on top. Remove this and make the counters free and clear of clutter, with two or so items on top, so it doesn't look sparse and unlived in, but also not lacking in space either.

In particular, pay attention to the kitchen cupboards. I currently have a very tiny kitchen, but in previous homes, I've had massive kitchens; the bigger the kitchen you give me, the more unorganized junk drawers I will have. So if you have cupboards where you can only open them an inch, and then everything will fall out on you, organize and declutter; you don't want people thinking there isn't enough storage. No buyer ever complained, "Ugh, this house has way too much storage for me."

And when I say declutter, I don't mean for you to move all that junk and shove it in the closets because—shocker and spoiler alert!—people will look inside (the closets as well). Gasp! How dare they? Now they might think there's not enough storage space for their stuff, when they see all your kitchen appliances spill out of the other closets.

I've had people put extra things in their home when selling in the dishwasher and stove and trying to declutter other spaces. However, people are going to open these appliances, since most likely, they are included in the purchase, or they want them to be. They open the dishwasher and see that you've shoved toilet paper rolls in there because you have no linen closet. Or they see your laundry supplies in your dishwasher because the closet where the washer and dryer are doesn't have space or is falling off its hinges and can't take the weight.

They'll soon realize the lack of storage, and instantly, their impression of the home begins to decline along with the purchase price they want to offer you—if they even offer, that is. Make sure you're not poorly hiding a flaw in the house, hide it properly by not bringing their attention to it. If the buyers don't notice there's no linen closet, then they don't notice. But it won't be because they discovered something stuffed and jammed where it doesn't belong.

Odours

Good or bad, smells can be overbearing, so aim for a scent-neutral home. I have a super-sensitive nose, so even good smells can be overwhelming for me and often give me a headache. Obviously, the bad smells we know are smoke, mold, pets, and even spices. But the good smells can be over the top, such as too many plugins or melted-wax kind of pots or air fresheners. Try to keep spaces clean and free with minimal scents. When there is a lot, even if you classify them as pleasant, many prospective buyers will think you're trying to mask or hide something.

Furniture

People are visual creatures. If they show up and see the house is a mess, one, they're going to reopen the listing on their phone and see if they're at the right address, and two, if it's vacant, they're going to have a harder time picturing furniture and how it all flows and comes together. I will always vote for real, live, touchable, sit-on-able staging as opposed to virtual staging. This is when you are shown a picture of living room furniture and dining room tables, but the furniture was never really in the house and isn't there for your viewing of the home.

If the rooms are small, make sure you're using properly scaled furniture, so it doesn't seem like a small room. If the ceilings are low, use lower furniture to not bring attention to the low height. If the space is awkward, make sure you show it as something, maybe it's an office or play space for kids. As I said, we are visual creatures, and many people have a hard time imagining spaces and furniture placement. You need to help them by imagining for them and bringing the home to life with physical staging—take the guesswork away for them.

Missing elements

If the house has a tiny landing and no closet (in some raised bungalows, for example), do not load the landing with shoes and a coatrack. Remove the coatrack to not draw attention to the fact there is no closet. Also, remove the shoes so they don't get a visual of the bomb that would happen if they lived there amid a pile of their kid's shoes.

Twice, I bought a home without a linen closet and didn't notice until I went to put my sheets and towels away. The second time I said, "Damnit, I did it again!" I hadn't checked for the linen closet that didn't exist. Sometimes I walk in the master bedroom closet of a listed home and see bedsheets and feminine hygiene products, and then I go back in the hall and realize there's no linen closet. If I hadn't seen that in the master bedroom walk-in closet, there's a much higher chance I wouldn't have noticed.

You don't want people to overanalyze the home and think there's not enough space or shine a light on the home's shortcomings. For example, your daughter's room is above the garage, and since it's freezing in there, you have a space heater during the winter. This may be the only way anyone would ever sleep in that room, but you don't need that out for showings if you're listed in the winter as it brings to the buyer's attention flaws in the home. Have it pumping full force right before the showing then in the last minute unplug it and move it to the garage or an unfinished tucked away space.

Details, details!

Be sure to go around your home and make a "honey-do" list. Check if any light bulbs are out, for example. Is there a hole in the wall where someone slammed the door too hard, and the handle broke the drywall? Could the caulking in the tub use a facelift? Say, the freezer doesn't work in your fridge. Don't have an extra chest freezer beside it in the kitchen, which is an eyesore and makes no sense. Get a new fridge, or have it repaired.

Prospective buyers will think that if you don't repair the little things, then you don't repair the big things. They will also often picture big price tags for repairs—and often wrong price tags as they don't know the costs. So make sure the property appears in its best light according to the guidelines I have mentioned. Clean up the inside and outside of the property, make sure nothing seems cluttered, do a deep cleaning, and make sure any touch-ups or honey-do lists are completed because potential buyers want to see pride of ownership.

Spruce up anything that needs to be remedied. Maybe your front door is quite dull and faded, so paint it. Maybe your carpeting in the basement smells like the litter of cats your daughter had downstairs and needs a powerful steam clean or to be ripped up and replaced. Maybe you need a couple of fresh coats of paint in some rooms or maybe even all the rooms in the house. Maybe you need a new roof or some shingles replaced. PS: if you're selling your home with a pool in the winter, make sure you include a picture of it in the summer. Do not have only summer pictures though, or the buyer might conclude that it's been for sale since the summer and try to lowball you!

Outdoor spaces

People also need help to envision the outdoor spaces. See if there is somewhere where you can create areas outside for people to hang out. Maybe one area is more casual with couches and a natural gas fire table or maybe chairs around a firepit or both, depending on the size of the yard. If you're targeting a family, and it's definitely not a bachelor's home, maybe a tree fort or a fun shed converted to play space is in your cards. Is there a place where you can hang a tire swing from a tree or those cool bucket chairs from a pergola?

Is there a deck outside? A patio space? Somewhere for people to hang out, have family over, let the kids play, and so forth? Is the space usable? Is it a cliff drop-off and scary to a family? Or is it a steep uphill so you're staring at a mound of dirt? You need to have functional space for people. Regardless of how nice you make the inside of the home, they do need to leave the home or they'll go stir crazy, so give them options. Remember quarantine? People just wanted to get out.

Don't show the backyard cluttered with furniture and children's toys. Create a simple area to sit or dine and remove the rest. You want people to see a clean space so they can imagine having friends over. You don't want them to think there's no room for entertaining and that the sellers have outgrown the house and that they're probably too big as a family for the property as well.

Similarly, if you're flipping or selling a condo, a play fort or structure is not going to make sense, and more of an entertainer vibe is needed. How big is the balcony? How can you make it the most functional for privacy and entertaining and essentially showing off a bit?

The mind is a powerful thing!

If my house isn't selling once I list it on the market, what should I do?

If you have a good realtor, he or she will inform you about everything you need to know and do. Be sure to engage a realtor in the top 1 percent in the area, but be careful to read the fine print. I've seen people advertise as the top 1 percent in the city where I live, and I know they're not, or I would have heard of them. If they were in the top 1 percent, I would have them, their partner, and their office numbers on speed dial because we would be doing deals together all the time.

They might advertise that they were the top 1 percent brokerage for sales, then you learn that was back in 2014. I've seen a brother-and-sister team advertise that they are the top 1 percent brother-and-sister team, when they were the only sister-and-brother team in the city—yet they only sell three to five homes a year. Or maybe they say they are in the top 1 percent at their brokerage when their brokerage only has three people.

When you hire a real estate agent, do your homework, and make sure they are in the top 1 percent of the region where they are practicing/licensed and measured against all other realtors—not just realtors under five foot two or with grey hair with pink highlights or their brokerage.

Real estate boards

In Canada, we have multiple real estate boards (even though the public thinks we only have realtor.ca). We have back end boards where realtors go and have a plenitude of extra criteria we can enter or request that our clients only be sent those. If an agent is not advertising on all applicable boards in the area, then he or she is not getting all available eyes on the property and not tapping into the full potential of a listing. The agent may have it listed for $500,000, and no one's biting, but if they list on two other boards at $549,000, suddenly, you could have a signed sealed and delivered offer for $540,000. Make sure you know which board(s) your home is listed on and if they are the proper ones to get you the best and most exposure possible.

Marketing

As you know, so much marketing is being done online. Besides all applicable boards, is the property being properly and efficiently marketed online? There are ways to list a property so it comes up while people are looking up other things on their mobile phones and laptops. Say, you look up a couch on Wayfair, and then on every page you visit afterward, you will see ads for that couch. Creepy? Yes. Effective? Definitely.

There's a way to be on the sites people visit, even if they haven't looked up something of yours in the first place. If that has been done, and it's been listed on the proper boards, and it's well-staged and showing in the best light and has professional photos and a virtual tour and still not selling, then you need to look at the bigger picture.

Is the agent using any Google analytics or behavioral targeting for your home or geofencing? What about Google ad words or Google pay-per-click? Is it in the paper (if that's still showing returns in your area—in many areas, the return on paper listings have completely died off)? Facebook? Instagram? On apps or YouTube commercials? Real estate isn't anywhere close to being what it was when your parents were buying and selling or depending on when you bought and sold last, when you were last in the game.

If the house doesn't sell, the next steps depend on whether the previous steps were taken. I wouldn't want someone reducing the listing price and taking potential profit off the table and out of their pockets when the house may be worth even more, and it's just not being listed in the right place so more people can see it.

Pricing

Are you listed for $500,000 when the homes similar to yours have been selling for much less? Are they selling in the low four-hundreds range? Well, that's a no-brainer and an easy fix if you're priced too high. If you think, "My house has granite and a walkout basement, and the others don't." Well, that will give you $5,000 for granite and $10,000 for the walkout, so you should be $444,900 or $449,000 max—you're sitting unsold because you're at least $50,000 overpriced.

Timing

Consider the time of year when you're listing if your house isn't selling. Where I'm located, the busiest time of the year is April,

May, and June, but this doesn't mean that's the best time to list, but that this is the time where there are the most homes to choose from. You will have the most competition as a seller, but it's handy to take advantage of the options as a buyer, assuming you will be on both sides of the equation. What if some of those properties are priced better than yours or have nicer finishes or are in a more desirable location? I like selling during the "off" seasons so I can have more of the upper hand.

Viewer feedback

If the price is right, then pay attention to what people have been saying when providing feedback after showings. Perhaps you have a neighbour that looks like he's having a yard sale out on his lawn, but he's not, and prospective buyers are turned off by the look of the junkyard next door. Perhaps you're walking distance to a jail, and they'd rather buy somewhere else for that reason. Maybe you're near a factory that gives off an awful smell and rings a bell once every half hour all day that echoes throughout the neighbourhood.

Cleanliness

Maybe the house itself has a bad odour. Has anyone commented on an odour or state of cleanliness? Does it smell like there's a dead mouse or a wet dog in the house? Are there layers of dirt on the baseboard, and you think the walls are an Easter-egg yellow, but in reality, they're white, and someone has been smoking inside for decades? I'm not even going to say what you need to do there, that's a given.

Staging

Let's revisit staging. How's the flow of the house? Do you have to shimmy past the couch and dining table because it's so tight in that area? Could you benefit from smaller furniture to match the space? Have you depersonalized the interior so people can look at the space instead of looking at the boudoir photoshoot you had done for your husband for your anniversary? Are there racks of clothes hanging in the master bedroom because the closet is so tiny? You don't want to bring attention to things not ideal in the home.

To sum up my list of options you have if your place isn't selling, be sure to examine all the things you can do. Don't automatically drop the price if your place isn't selling. Look at how and where it's been marketed and advertised, compare pricing, and evaluate the condition of your home and how it shows to others.

Make sure everything is functioning properly. Not every buyer is going to test every item in your home, but the serious ones will—and not necessarily and most likely not during the showing but during the home inspection. For example, I was at a home recently and saw that there was a fork on the side of the tub. I asked, "Were you eating something tasty in there?"

He replied, "The faucet doesn't work so you need a fork to pull this mechanism on the back."

Ugh, why didn't you replace the faucet before showing the house!?

Part 5

Landlording

Landlords grow rich in their sleep without working,
risking or economizing.
—John Stuart Mill, political economist

The most important aspect of being a landlord is being relaxed and not getting stressed out. If you get stressed easily, then being a landlord might not be the best career choice for you. Hands down. End of discussion. Shit happens, and things go wrong. Emergencies pop up, and you need to be ready to roll with it.

If you're determined to join the landlording game, I suggest you don't have a short temper. Don't have an ego. Don't talk down to people. Just be a regular approachable person. I've found that when dealing with tenants, if I act as a property manager or the realtor acting on behalf of the property rather than the owner, I can pass the blame onto an unknown, fake person (the "owner") if I need to serve them papers or have difficult conversations or enforce rules they may not agree with.

What are a landlord's responsibilities when it comes to caring for their properties? Are there any laws that define these?

It goes without saying that your local laws will trump anything I write here. So I will say once again that you should do your homework and know the governance of your specific jurisdiction. Following is a general overview of what you will need to investigate for your area.

Zoning, codes, and safety standards

Standards can vary, depending upon your municipality's laws; however, there are some general rules of thumb. Your rental must meet your jurisdiction's building code and safety standards. The landlord must comply with zoning. If your property is zoned to be a bank, for example, you can't make it an eighteen-bedroom rooming house and use all the bank offices or cubicles for different tenants. I call the vault! (Actually, no, I don't; I'd be afraid to get locked in and was slightly claustrophobic as a child. I didn't like elevators or bathrooms where the stall doors went right to the ground either.)

There's also a basic level of health, safety, and maintenance you need to follow. The apartment or complex must be in a good state of repair. I don't know if this "good state" is documented anywhere. Heck, as a teenager, I lived at an apartment with cockroaches that was far from good, if you ask me. Many things about rentals seem to depend on the by-law person who shows up and what kind of mood he or she is in—there are lots of grey areas. I had an officer tell me, "Well, you don't have to get a survey, but we would prefer that you did."

I asked, "But it's not mandatory?"

"No, but we prefer that you did it anyway."

Well, I'm not going to shell out $1,300 to $1,600 for something I don't have to.

Another time, I was trying to find out about adding a unit, and I was told, "It's a grey area."

I asked, "How so?"

He said, "Well, I like to talk in traffic lights, and you're a yellow teetering on red."

I said I had no issue with that, but I asked if there was somewhere I could read what is and isn't allowed.

He said, "No, it's more of an unspoken rule."

Well, either you can or can't—not all this *grey-area unspoken-rule* bullshit. I'll ask for forgiveness instead of permission, thank you very much.

Of course, there are off-the-grid homes, but for the "norm," there would also have to be utilities, such as electricity, gas, and water available for the tenants hook up with their own accounts unless the landlord is paying the utilities.

Reasonable, quiet, and peaceful enjoyment

There have been a few times I've been in the courtroom, and I hear arguments about *reasonable enjoyment*, which can also be called quiet enjoyment or peaceful enjoyment.

These terms refer to the right of an occupant to enjoy and use premises in peace and without interference. Quiet enjoyment is often an implied condition in a lease. The term *quiet* is not restricted to the absence of noise but interpreted as uninterrupted enjoyment of their property. This rule is also an umbrella for smoke. So if one tenant is smoking in a unit, the other tenant can complain as their right to reasonable enjoyment of their unit has been violated.

This right for a tenant also covers harassment from the landlord and any silly rules the landlord might have such as not permitting guests to stay over. I was looking for a new apartment in Toronto when I was younger, and I found one that was something crazy cheap. I said to myself that I didn't care what it was like, and as long as it didn't have cockroaches, I was in.

It was a private bedroom with a shared living and dining room. The lady was in her nineties, and when I arrived to look at the place, she said if I took the room, I was allowed no visitors and that included anyone I was dating, friends, and parents. She also said I had to be in at 8:00 pm every night. Well, I was a bartender who worked until 3:30 or 4:00 a.m., so that didn't work. *Damn!* I had been calculating all the money I would save if my monthly caring costs were that cheap. As they say, if it sounds too good to be true, it probably is.

Another way a landlord can compromise a tenant's right to quiet enjoyment is by not repairing things in the unit that are safety issues or trying to force a tenant to sign something they don't understand or don't want to. This would breach the tenant's right to peaceful enjoyment without interference.

If one tenant is ruining another tenant's right to quiet enjoyment (or smoke-free enjoyment), it's the landlord's responsibility to take care of it. As a tenant or a landlord, I recommend that you keep good records of any breaches as this will be very handy if the issue ever goes to court.

Selling personal items in exchange for rent

Also, in residential (not commercial) properties, a landlord is not allowed to sell anything that the tenant owns to go toward rent. For example, if the tenant is late in paying rent, the landlord can't go to the home and take their child's little remote control jeep or the lawnmower and sell it on Craigslist to go towards their rent.

How do I decide what will be my responsibilities, and what will be the tenants'?

The tenant has general responsibilities, such as they must pay their rent on time and in full each month. They must behave well and repair any damage caused by neglect. They must allow entry to a unit for showings if the home is for sale, or their lease is ending, and they are given proper notice for those viewings or for repairs or yearly maintenance, etc. Most places require a minimum of twenty-four-hour notice.

They can't harass the landlord. I had one tenant call me nine times in a row. I was on an important call and called her right back and asked, "What's the problem?"

She said, "There's a grasshopper in my bedroom."

I wanted to say, "Well, that's lovely lady—but why are you calling me like a crazy ex?"

I put in my leases that any repair or maintenance under $100 is the responsibility of the tenant. Otherwise, I find that tenants call and say that the furnace isn't working when the thermostat just needed new batteries. Or they'll call and say that the air conditioner isn't working when the breaker is just in the wrong position. Or they have ants and want an exterminator when Dollar Store ant traps will do the job.

I also want my tenants to be responsible for replacing the light bulbs in their unit and batteries in the smoke detectors. If the appliances or the furnace breaks, I will cover it for normal wear and tear—but not if they ripped the door off or something ridiculous.

Some tenants think they live in the Taj Mahal, so my advice is not to fix every little thing, or you'll never hear the end of it. Usually, you can tell when showing the property what kind of tenant they'll be when they ask questions such as "Is that going to be fixed? Can you hear the road a lot? Will the landlord come and clean that? Can I park my trailer and three boats on the property?"

Watch for those red flags, and don't let them move in in the first place. My places are gorgeous and not dives by any means, and I get plumbing and appliances fixed, but if they say there's an indent in that baseboard, or if they have to turn the nozzle to the left for cold water instead of the right—that's not being fixed. (If you don't like it, go buy your own house or rent somewhere else. *Sorry not sorry.*)

It's the same with tenants who say the light isn't working and they need an electrician ASAP as they work from home and can't go without light. And then you find out either a) the breaker is just flipped or b) the bulb is out. (It's normally option b.) Don't immediately send someone expensive for a repair when often a repair is something small that can be dealt with cheaply and often yourself.

Your lease will state who pays which utilities. Ordinarily, everything is the landlord's responsibility other than damage to the property caused by the tenant. You're not going to have a tenant pay to have your eaves troughs (or gutters in the States) cleaned, for example. You also aren't going to have a tenant pay for new shingles on the roof. But if a tenant decides to steam clean the laminate flooring and wrecks it—as I mentioned happened to me—then the cost falls on them. Or if a tenant punches a hole in the wall or causes other damage, they are responsible for the repairs.

Who is responsible for landscaping and yard work?

In your leases, be sure to detail who is cutting the grass, salting the driveway, and all other regular maintenance responsibilities. Perhaps you could say that the rent is $1,800, or it will be $1,900 including snow and grass maintenance. Where I live, it's quite customary for the tenant to take responsibility for the lawn and snow maintenance. However, if they don't keep up with their obligations, and the property starts to look rough or sketchy, I will be held responsible—not the tenants—regardless of what the lease says. If a neighbour calls to report the property, then by-law will come out to the property and issue a fine to me. I would rather pay a lawn maintenance company or some local teenager twenty or thirty dollars and save myself from by-law snooping around the property.

I am definitely not a gardener—the green thumb of my mom and grandma skipped me and died at me, I suppose—so I don't have landscaping at my properties. I pay for the grass to be cut and the snow to be ploughed. I let the leaves disintegrate. I have one pool at present, and I pay for people to come twice a week to vacuum and shock it and make sure it's clean. That property also has a lot of rosebushes, so I do have someone take care of them; otherwise, they attack people when they come to the front door. That unit is an Airbnb now, but if I were renting it out long-term, I'd have the tenant deal with it. Besides that property, I don't have any with flower beds as the likeliness of tenants keeping up with it is slim to none, and I don't want to pay a gardener.

Should I cultivate relationships with my tenants? (The relationships could be friendship or romance or business-related.)

I have not had any luck in this department, so I'm saying no, no, and no yet again. I've had staff live in my houses, and then they start slacking off, but when I want to fire them, it gets complicated because now, they're in one of my homes. I've had siblings of contractors in my units, and then the contractors screw me over, and the siblings stop paying rent. I had clients stay in one of my rentals as they waited to go to their newly built house, which ended up getting bedbugs, and I felt horrible. I dated someone at one of my properties, and when we broke up, we were much too intertwined, and that never ends well, as you can guess.

When you have friendships, business relationships, or dating relationships with tenants, they always think you will be lenient with them. Well, the bank isn't lenient with me, so I can't say, "Sorry, Bank, can we cuddle so I don't have to pay this months' mortgage payment?" or "It's been a tough month with everything lately, Bank. Can we skip a few months since we're besties and all?" The bank doesn't care—I still owe what I owe. Unfortunately, people tend to think that since you're friends, the same paying rules don't apply to them.

Personal relationships with tenants should never go deep because you'll often get screwed in the end. In one case, I had a friend who wanted to stay for two months for free while they got their "feet on the ground." Well, that turned into having animal feces everywhere in the apartment, destroying all the staged furniture in the unit, and punching holes in the walls. Yay—so glad I did a favour for someone I know and will now never speak to again.

I don't want you to think that the rental game is all unpaying trashing people. Usually, the tenants take better care of the properties than I do, to be honest. I'm never home, often working, or travelling, so gardening and home upkeep are not on any of my to-do lists. As I mentioned, I'm not a gardener. I've had tenants add gardens, add a firepit, take care of the leaves, and do some interlocking. I had one tenant do risers and paint the stairs, and they looked great. She sent me before-and-after pictures, and I said, "That looks great! How much do I owe you?"

She said, "Don't worry about it. You're a great landlord."

If they think you're a dick, they'll try to screw you. So when I say don't go too deep, it doesn't mean you have to be rude to them, but just don't get super close. Do not fall for the cuteness of their kids. Definitely do not exchange holiday gifts with them. Do not be at their beck and call. Let the phone ring, let it go to voicemail, and if it's time sensitive, call them right back.

Should I hire a local property management company?

If you're looking to hire a property manager, do your homework. Check their reviews. Check how many clients they've had. Do they work with hundreds of clients, or are you their first? Make sure they're reputable, have tons of reviews, and have preferably been referred by a friend or two who has used their services.

You should also shop call them. Randomly call them from a different number and pretend that you're a tenant looking to rent the property and see what they say. If you can, have a friend go in person, and ask if the owner keeps up the building and how professional they are. Also, check about side deals. See if you could move in early for cheaper rent in cash. I've seen property managers say a tenant didn't rent until the first of October, but meanwhile, someone was in there since September and giving them cash on the side. A reputable property management company is not going to risk their license, reputation, and name for a few bucks, but someone who has nothing to lose will.

You'd be surprised how many people ask me to do things against our code of ethics, some offering $500 and others $10,000. Why would I risk everything and not have a job anymore for that amount of money? That makes no sense to me. However, a property manager that doesn't have clients and doesn't care if they could lose something could take the bait.

Should I be on a maintenance plan to fix and repair things?

For yearly long-term rentals, I would say, on average, one repair occurrence happens per year. Sometimes it's a broken faucet or appliance, part of a fence falls in a windstorm, or a tenant locks themselves out. With short-term rentals, things happen more often, which makes sense since there is more traffic, and you're getting a higher return. A higher return means a higher chance that there may be issues; it comes hand in hand.

With short-term rentals, I don't repair things more often, but I do have to get new sheets, towels, and sometimes they will steal things such as bathrobes or throw pillows. I've had a kitchen repainted because it was peeling. I've also redone a floor beaten up from a combination of kids riding around on bikes and roller skates and pushing things inside, but I haven't had to repair anything that didn't make the investment worth it. It's often hard to do repairs in short-term rentals as they're constantly rented (if you've priced properly, of course). Some owners will block off time to do the tweaks, and others will just let the cash come in.

Finding Renters

Obviously, a key aspect to successful landlording is having great tenants. But how do you choose from what hopefully will be a lot of applicants? And where do you find tenants? It seems every month there's four if not more new sites for renters and buyers to connect. At the time of this printing, I am using Facebook Marketplace to advertise, although in the past, I've used Kijiji and Craigslist.

I suggest that you set a day or two maximum to be at the property for a one-hour window. During that time, you can hold an open house where potential renters come in, and you can get a feel for them, have a chat, and hand out applications if requested. If you offer only one time slot per tenant, and they don't show up, you are going to be super frustrated and waste a lot of time. If you offer an hour and book thirty prospective tenants and only six show up, then it doesn't matter if the others didn't show. At least you will have six potential tenants.

Whoever does show up and expresses an interest in the property, have them fill out an application, get their credit rating, letter of employment, and a copy of two pay stubs. If all lines up, they sign a lease, give you first and last month's rent, and you won't hear from them (knock on wood) more than once per year.

Note: if they tell you horror stories about the previous landlord and how she or he didn't do this or that, don't rent to them—they're bad news waiting to happen, no matter how much their previous landlord seems like an ass.

What qualities should I look for in a renter?

I visually assess my prospective tenants. When we meet, I write something on their paper (which now I won't be able to do since I'm giving it away). I write the numbers 110 on the back. People think, "Cool, I got over a hundred, so I must be pretty spiffy!" But if you connect the one *1* to the other number *1* from upper left to lower bottom right, it spells "NO." That was something my boss used to do when I bartended and waitressed, so I just brought it into my rentals also.

I will meet all potential tenants, but I prefer young couples moving out of their parents' house and in with each other. They usually have decent jobs and a lot of school debt. There's a good chance they will need to rent for two to five years, which is handy for a lack of turnover.

I have many interesting stories about the potential renters who have walked through my doors over the years. One fellow came in with a bloody nose, a black eye, and a tampon stuck up his nose. He was also very drunk, but luckily, he was not driving and arrived on a bicycle, which still probably wasn't the safest situation.

(Yes, I scored him 110.)

I had a woman show up with five children to view a 480-square-foot one-bedroom apartment. I asked, "You have how many kids? You realize this is a one-bedroom?"

She responded, "This unit is bigger than the one I have now. They'll share a room, and I'll sleep on the couch."

(110.)

One fellow asked to trade sexual favors for rent.

(You guessed it: 110. And WTF buddy? Am I on a hidden prank show?)

I rented rooms out at one home, and since I lived thirty minutes out of the city, and as one fellow worked from home, he would watch my dog for me. Anyways, I arrived one day to pick up my dog and found a group of women sitting in the living room and kitchen. They weren't speaking to each other like they were friends, and there was no partying going on, just an awkward tension. He wasn't the most popular of fellows, so all these pretty women saying they were waiting for him was quite odd. I went upstairs, and my handsome puppy greeted me in the hallway.

I knocked on the fellow's door, and he opened it an inch. "Hey," I said, "What's going on with all the women downstairs?" Turns out there's a whole market for foot photography. He would pay women to take pictures of their feet in different shoes, then he would make multiple copies and sell them on some site.

Who knew?! My virgin ears and feet.

What are some red flags in a potential renter that should let me know not to rent to that person?

Aside from the couple of scenarios I listed above, the massive and obvious red flag is their wage. You would be surprised how many people write that they make $2,000 a month but apply to rent a $2,300-a-month house. I'll acknowledge their application if it's in person to me. I'll say, "I don't quite understand how you will be able to pay the rent though John Doe plus make up the difference for groceries, gas, your car payment, etc.?" They usually look like a deer in the headlights and perhaps think I can't do simple math.

Another thing they do when applying is to complain, "My current landlord never fixes anything. The toilet hasn't worked, and they're noisy upstairs, and there's mold in the shower and a broken window." They mention all the issues. Sometimes they'll mention that they're taking the landlord to court, and that's why they're moving. Maybe they think it's good to be open, but

I would definitely not rent to these people who complain about having landlord-tenant issues.

I've also had people say they have no credit at all, and they've never had a credit card. They explain that there's no point in showing a credit report. This is most certainly not the case, as it's usually that they have an extremely low and unflattering credit score.

If you want to go through your applications with a fine-toothed comb if you're going to be paying utilities, there are other things to think about. Do they have multiple little ones (so lots of baths)? Do they have three cars and a boat? You can decide at that point if you want to go for the couple with one car and no dependents (if you have a bunch of applicants to choose from) or take a chance on a bigger family with more stuff. I know who I'd pick.

However, if they pay for their own utilities, then you won't care about that part, but there will be more wear and tear in the one scenario more than likely over the other.

I also don't like if they're self-employed as they can claim to make $3,000 a month, and maybe they show you a cheque or deposit for that, but maybe they only had that one and no other jobs that whole year. Depending on where a landlord is located, they may be allowed to ask for bank account history (but it's not a common practise).

There's a super-detailed site called Naborly. I know a dozen or so investors who rent units out but live out of town or city and don't use property managers. They will ask prospective tenants to log on to the site and answer a boatload of questions, and then the site will give the owner the results. This way they only drive in to show the unit to people with a high score.

How are short-term renters (like Airbnb guests) different from long-term renters?

Short-term renters can be people from other countries coming to visit a major metropolitan city and are usually a solo person or a couple or two friends sharing a space. They are usually doing the typical sightseeing stuff. You'll also get conference attendees (depending on the city) and the odd local doing a girl's night away or anniversary celebration.

Then if you have a short-term rental out of a major city, you normally get the local city people trying to get out of the hustle and bustle. I've seen people come up to ski, celebrate anniversaries, go for nights away with friends, see a concert, and hold baby gender reveals. I've had people get ready multiple times the night before their wedding, but the norm is a night away from the city. The nonlocals from other countries usually visit the major metropolitan areas, then the residences of the metropolitan homes/condos and so forth go to the cottages and houses out of town for getaways.

Long-term tenants are looking for homes. They care more than a short-term renter about the size of the yard and the functionality of the kitchen. They care if there is a school close by for their kids, enough parking spots, and so forth. Short-term renters don't care if they have to park on the street or if the kitchen layout isn't ideal for holiday cooking, etc. Long-term tenants will look where laundry is, and they will check closet sizes.

Do you have any advice on how I should handle troublesome short-term renters?

There's a general rule of thumb for best return to least return; however, the scale of problem and annoyance goes the same way. I like Airbnb's insurance. I like the idea of them taking care of it and being done with those potential "bad" visitors in a short-term rental situation as opposed to going through the whole system and process of eviction with the sheriff and court. If they're visiting short term and pose a problem, done and done, bye! (No waiting for sheriffs for weeks or months.)

For short-term rentals, I suggest you maintain a file for all the receipts of what is in the house, such as couches, lamps, throw pillows, bathrobes, etc. If a guest wrecks something in the short-term rental, you can quickly reference it. Airbnb doesn't like to do anything without an invoice. I give all my receipts to my accountant, so if anything happens, I have to ask him, and he has one of his helpers look for it (and they charge me), which obviously doesn't make sense, but it's all learning. In the future, I wouldn't do it that way again. It's only a failure if you don't learn anything!

When you're made aware of a severe problem, contact the guest. If they don't respond or stop the behavior, call Airbnb or whichever platform you're using. Airbnb will reach out to them, and if they can't get a hold of them, with the owner's permission, they will cancel the reservation. Then if you are so inclined, you can call the police.

Make sure to lock everything up! Not like the bed and couch, but all the extras. If you shop at a bulk store, such as Costco or Walmart, do not make extra toilet paper, paper towels, and other supplies accessible to the guests as some will take your extra stock. Suddenly, you have no dish soap when you just put out eight bottles, and there's no shampoo, and you just put out six extras. A simple lock on a closet door that has all these extras solves the problem. It sounds silly, but guests do often take your extras. Cheeky buggers.

Do I put any clauses in my leases to make it easier to get a bad renter out of the property if they're doing something destructive or dangerous?

In Ontario, you're not allowed to evict someone for doing something dangerous. You can give them notice if you see destruction to the property caused by their animal; however, you can't shorten their stay because of a clause you added to the lease. There are set rules and time frames for getting people out for things such as paying the rent late or never, but the owner can't decide what that window is, it's set out legislatively.

The question of rent

How do I know if I'm asking the right price?

The market will tell you if you're too high. If sixty people come through, and not one asks for an application, then you're too high. If only three come through, and one fills out an application, and you just don't like them as tenants, you're most likely fine. I would hold another day of viewings and then decide.

Check out your competition (the other rentals available) and solds (leased-out properties). Were they super nice and asking

$500 less per month? Then you are up shit's creek with your pricing.

In the beginning, when I didn't know rents inside and out, I'd go online, check out my competition, and price my unit based on the other listings. I usually tried to push the envelope to price on the high-end for the number of bedrooms, which weeded out those who couldn't afford my asking price. Also, a higher price generally gives you a better batch from which to choose.

The most important thing to consider when deciding what to charge for rent is to see that you've covered your expenses. You don't want to charge $1,000 a month if your mortgage is $1,200, plus you have property tax, utilities (if the renter isn't paying their own), insurance, and miscellaneous repairs such as when a fridge breaks.

I never bought a property that didn't make financial sense for me. I never worried about charging low rents to attract tenants. I always have made my places visually appealing to the eye, so finding renters has never been an issue, nor asking market or higher than market rent.

As an investor, I always wanted to make 10 percent or more, but some people might wish to make 15 percent or only 6 percent, so it changes according to what makes sense for each investor. Did I pull my number out of thin air back in the day? Yep, pretty much. I saw what the bank was giving me—or not giving me, I should say—so 10 percent seemed like an excellent return to me. I had some properties that returned over 30 percent, and some that were right over the line at 10.1 percent. But as long as it was over 10 percent, I was happy and had my little "real estate high."

If I put down $60,000 on a home and spent $20,000 in renovations, I'm in it for $80,000. Ten percent of that is $8,000, so I want a minimum return of $8,000 a year (not counting the home's appreciation, or how much my mortgage/principal is going down). So $8,000 divided by twelve months is $666.67, so I need to be clearing on top of all my expenses at least that amount for me even to consider that purchase. Sometimes they return 20 to 25 percent, but that's my minimum. Also, when I came up with this figure before, it was from long-term rentals, which return less, so it's much easier now to profit with short-term rentals.

How do I determine the security deposit amount?

I charge first and last month's rent, and that's it. I know that's not exciting, but it's truthful. Although I don't ask for a security deposit, I have my tenants pay their last month's rent when they know they're moving even though I have already collected it up front. When we do the final walkthrough together, if I find everything to be satisfactory, I return the last month's rent I have been holding. If there are damages, then the last month's rent goes toward fixing whatever was damaged. If there is any leftover, I will give it back to them.

Should I allow pets and charge pet rent?

In the city I live in, there's a limit of two dogs per household, but who knows if anyone enforces that law unless you have a neighbour who hates you and continuously calls by-law on you.

Ninety percent of landlords where I live don't allow pets. I've had one issue in all my properties regarding pets, so I allow them, which gets people excited and willing to pay more since they've been turned down at so many other places.

I don't charge a pet deposit or pet rent. Besides not wanting cats for a bit, I don't discriminate against pets. Almost 75% of the people in the city where I live who rent have pets, so if I say no to them, I am making my pool of renters that much smaller. Because none of my units have carpet, I don't see it as an issue, or at least not a big enough of an issue to prevent me from renting to pet owners. I'm a dog lover through and through, so I can't discriminate against my handsome friends.

One potential tenant had three cats, and I didn't want to rent to them after I'd had a recent bad experience with cats. However, they swore up and down that their cats wouldn't be a problem. I turned them down but didn't tell them it was because of the cats. However, they came to another rental of mine a few weeks later and recognized me. They filled out all the paperwork again, and I told them I didn't want to waste their time and that the "landlord" wasn't keen on cats. They offered to pay one full month's rent extra if they were allowed to move in with the cats, so I allowed it.

Should I include utilities? What about things like trash pickup and water?

If you think that utilities are going to be an issue or that people will not be cautious with their usage, state in the lease that utilities are included, but any amount over a specific price will be the responsibility of the tenant. Tenants will be less likely to be wasteful and will turn off lights and not crank the air conditioner in February. They tend to be more careful if they know they will be responsible for any excessive bills.

Most of my units include heat, hydro, and water, but they don't include internet or cable. (Actually, that's a lie. My short-term rentals have Internet.) I don't do cable, but there are smart TVs at the properties. Only one unit in my history has not included utilities. Since I have so many multiple units, I found that people would complain even if the apartments were identical in size. They'd say the other tenants have a bath every night or take longer showers and that they use less water and are conscientious with the lights, and the other tenants are not, therefore they don't want to split the bills with them.

It was annoying, so I began to advertise differently. For example, let's say I wanted $1,800 in rent. I would offer either $1,725 plus utilities, which was not the actual price it would be, or $1,800 including heat, hydro, and water. Nearly everyone chooses the higher amount and I did that on purpose just to get things the way I wanted. If it was actually plus utilities, I probably would have asked for $1,550 or $1,600, but because I didn't want that option, I made the higher price seem like a no-brainer. There isn't a way to separate the services in most of my places, but I do it to grab their attention with the cheaper rent amount. I also include grass and snow maintenance, since when they offer to do it themselves, they tend not to do it at all, and then the neighbours complain. Too many times receiving calls from the neighbours about the tenants' lack of upkeep and me rolling my eyes mean I now just build it into my cost and take care of it on my end.

Are there any laws or regulations a landlord must be aware of around rental rates?

Laws and regulations will be specific to your neck of the woods, so you'll have to check into the specifics. To give you some examples of what you need to know, I will discuss Ontario, where I live.

I have never raised anyone's rent before. I always let people stay at their initial rental amount for as long as they reside at my property. I find that many people tend to go on to buy a home afterward, so I'm fine if they stay for a long time. I prefer not getting a few extra bucks to avoid having to take time to show the unit to prospective tenants year after year. Instead, I keep the current renters.

In Ontario, you must wait twelve months after the tenant moves in to up their rent. Let's say I rented it for $1,400 a month for three years. When those tenants moved out, I would assess and see if it was still worth $1,400 or if I should ask for $1,625 at that point. When the home is vacant, you can ask for whatever rent you want and don't have to follow the guideline. It's only when tenants are in the unit/home that you need to follow them.

If you're going to raise your tenant's monthly rent in Ontario, you must give them three months' written notice before you take action. In 2018 and 2019, the maximum increase was 1.8 percent, and in 2020, the maximum rental increase allowed is 2.2 percent. If you're charging $1,500 per month ($1500 x 0.022 = $33), you could go up to $1,533 per month for the next year.

For those who qualify for government-subsidized housing, then a raise of 2.2 percent for 2020, for example, is not applicable. Subsidized housing is generally based on family size and household income instead of the market rate.

Also, don't shoot the messenger, as I don't make the rules, but the 2.2 percent doesn't apply if your building, mobile home, or land lease community was built after November 15, 2018. If you have a self-contained unit in a home that has two or fewer units, and they were built after the noted date, you are most likely not protected under this rule, which means the landlord could raise the rent 10 percent, 50 percent, or whatever they desire.

Also, unfortunately for tenants, you're not covered if you share the kitchen or bathroom with the landlord. If you move in and agree to pay $500 a month, and two months later, he/she wants to raise it to $600, they can, and two months after that, they can raise it again. This is legal, but don't ask me why. Since this book is geared for landlords or those wanting to be landlords and not tenants, maybe you like this rule.

There's also an application called an L5 that a landlord can file to ask to raise the rent, then the set yearly guideline (like the 2.2 percent example). The landlord can apply if the municipal taxes have gone up significantly, or he/she has done a significant renovation or repair, or lastly, if they have experienced high operating costs due to security measures. The L5 must be filed ninety days before the landlord intends to up the rent, and the tenant must have it thirty or more days before the court/trial hearing.

The extra renovation work must have been completed within eighteen months before the request; the landlord can't say that eight years ago she/he renovated and now wants to up the tenant's rent $900 a month. Although you can ask for more than 2.2 percent (for example, since that is current, but please seek consultation regarding your area and year to be precise), you can't just tack on 50 percent. Landlords can only go up an additional 3 percent for capital expenditures or security services in Ontario.

One of the many reasons I don't raise the rent is the useful life of the capital expenditure. Does this sound confusing? Let me explain. Let's say I redo the kitchen, and at the hearing, the judge says it gives an added value to the house for eight years, and the tenant lives there for another ten. Then I'm allowed to charge them more rent for eight years, but then I'll need to reduce it for the last two years. This is just too complicated and silly in my opinion. That's why I don't ever do that.

I had a DT (design technology/shop) teacher when I was in grade 6, and he said he liked the KISS method, which is keep it simple stupid. Why complicate it with adding twenty bucks here and there or filling out forms and going to court to add $50 for a few years only to bring it back down again?

I do renovations when I first buy a property when no one lives there, not while they live there. When they move out, and I decide I want to do something else, then I will charge more rent but not while they're there. Otherwise, I will have to jump through all these hoops for the board. That's just me, but everyone can do as they feel comfortable.

What are some strategies to maximize the rent potential in a specific property?

The more units or bedrooms you have, the more rent you can collect. Obviously, a four-bedroom home is going to rent for more than a bachelor or studio apartment. If there's a way to do so, you can add extra rooms. For example, if you have a large open space, perhaps you could divide it and add an extra bedroom.

One of my properties is for sale right now. When I purchased it, it was a single-family house with a main-floor bedroom and upper-floor bedroom and one bathroom. I turned the front huge formal living/dining room into two more bedrooms, as there was already another living/dining room. In the back, where there had been a bedroom, I added an extra door and changed the bedroom to a kitchen and bathroom. I used the upstairs bedroom as a bedroom/living room and blocked off the units, so now there were two.

Then the stairs were going the wrong way for making a third unit, so I had them flipped around and added another entry door and made a two-bedroom basement apartment. That only required adding a kitchen in a rec room, as the bedrooms and full bathroom were already down there.

The more units you have, the more rent you can pull in, and the more bedrooms they have, the higher the rent you can charge. Speaking of bedrooms, I personally like one and two-bedroom units the best. I know I just said about more bedrooms, but hear me out. I like them because I can rent to young couples before they buy their first home. I found that multiple bedroom homes attract families, and I have better luck with couples. But you could test this in your area and see what's better for your market.

The nicer your unit is, the more rent you can collect. I want everything painted crisply and nice—not one room red, one purple, one green, and one blue. I always provide stainless steel appliances. I don't like linoleum floors, so I always cover them with tile. I'm not the biggest fan of carpet and will have it removed. I usually change the light fixtures and window coverings if they're super ugly. Preparing for a tenant is like preparing to flip, so think about whatever will make a tenant want to rent your place over the competition.

What kind of excuses will I hear from those who are late on their rent or can't pay, and how should I handle them?

You'll hear everything you can imagine!

New job and not paid yet.

They're sick.

Their parents are ill or passed.

Their child is ill so they can't work.

Their dog had to go to the vet.

Their car needed new brakes.

You know that saying about giving an inch, and they'll take a mile? It's true. Once they know you aren't a hard ass, if they're a little late, they'll keep pushing for later and later and smaller and smaller amounts. My advice is to be strict with your warnings and evictions, or they'll walk all over you. However, if you do your homework in the first place, you're less likely to have any issues with your tenants.

Besides one tenant I have right now who's always late but has lived there for years, I have no one else behind, and more than half of my tenants usually pay me before the first of the month. Sometimes they call and say, "It's the sixth of the month. Were you going to come by and get the rent?" Sometimes I forget, that's why I like e-transfer better because you press one button, and—voilà—there's rent in your bank account, as opposed to driving all over to pick it up or getting cheques that could bounce.

Leasing Life

What should I include in a lease?

The absolute minimum that should go in a lease includes the date, the tenant's name, my name (I always act as the landlord and not the owner), the address, the length of the lease, and the amount they will pay per month. It also includes whether the first and last month's rent will be paid up front.

You should lay out who's responsible for which utility bill because the last thing you need is for the tenants to call you and say they have no power. When you call the utility company, you learn that neither you nor they had been paying the bills, and now the power has been disconnected. You'll then need to reinstate the account and address, and there most likely will be a hookup fee, and possibly, your credit has been dinged.

Include who is responsible for grass cutting and snow removal. You don't want to be stuck paying for snow removal when they said they would do it in exchange for cheaper rent. Now you don't have it documented anywhere; they're getting more affordable rent, and you're stuck hiring an outside company.

If the area is commonly patrolled by by-law officers, I include that I'm not responsible for any parking tickets. You would be surprised what tenants ask from you. It is not my fault if you had a party, and all your friends didn't pay for street parking and received tickets—I'm not covering parking tickets, nice try.

I have never had anyone switch out my appliances, such as changing out my stainless-steel stove for a 1970s green model. But I always write in that the existing appliances remain in the unit and list each one. You can never be too careful.

I ask that the tenants get renter's insurance. I have insurance that covers flood, fire, and so forth. However, if a tree falls on the house and wrecks their wedding dress or some fancy art sculpture, then that claim goes on their insurance (not mine) for the dress and artwork (my insurance will cover the roof and walls, etc.). I don't expect people who rent from me to have the Mona Lisa hanging in their living room, but better safe than sorry. Also, if the basement floods, and they need to go to a hotel for a week, it's on their insurance, not out of pocket for me. Make sure they have their insurance and sign off that they have it, or know that they have been told they should get it and have chosen not to do so.

I always include in my leases that after a year, they revert to a monthly lease. While I could have them sign another contract, I let them live there for as long as they want. The longer they live there, the fewer times I have to show the unit to potential tenants, so it's a win-win as far as I'm concerned. Also, if I decide to sell the property, then it's easier to get them out if they're on month to month as opposed to a year lease.

I always write that there is no smoking allowed in the unit. I also specify how many parking spots are included with the unit. If there are ten spots in the back, and I don't say which specific ones are included, the next thing I know, they'll have two vehicles and a work truck, a trailer with a flat tire, a snowmobile and a motorcycle. My advice is to be specific; otherwise, it's your word against theirs in court.

If the property has coin laundry, then I'll include that in the lease. Otherwise, they'll say they didn't know and ask for money off the rent every month, which is super annoying. I had a tenant request seventy-five dollars off the rent each month because she didn't know she had to pay for laundry. I told her from the beginning, but because it wasn't on paper anywhere, she said it was the first time she'd heard of it.

Additionally, in writing, I get them to acknowledge that there are smoke and carbon monoxide detectors (and a fire extinguisher, if applicable). The last thing I want is for the house to burn down because the tenants removed my equipment, and for my insurance to deny the claim because there were no detectors. By including these items on the lease, I have proof they were there at the onset of the lease.

I also make them acknowledge that they will change the furnace filter, whether provided by them or me. As you probably could guess, there's a much better chance it will get done if you were to drop it off than rely on them to get one. In the past, I also dropped a container of salt for the snow, but this is obviously dependent on the climate where the property is located.

I also include a note about the use of the unit. For example, I stipulate that it is residential and is not meant for commercial use. I don't need anyone trying to run a business out of their basement apartment (even though I do appreciate their hustle).

As a landlord, you should address subleasing, as well as who is living on the property. You don't want to rent to tenants and specify that you will be paying the utilities when you think a couple is moving in, and then eight more people move in.

If you take cheques—and not cash or e-transfer—but a cheque bounces, who is responsible for the NSF fee or charge? Also, I've seen people put in leases that if rent is not paid on the first of every month, there will be an additional $200 fee for late payment. I have not done this, but it would be nice.

Also mention in your lease that any alterations, such as painting or decorating, needs to be approved by the landlord first. I had one tenant paint the walls and ceilings black. That was fun to paint over afterward—not!

When I was less than ten, my mom painted our kitchen fuchsia, and my grandmother painted hers lavender purple—both in rented kitchens. Those were probably some angry landlords. My grandma even got appliance paint and painted the fridge and stove lavender and then painted her ceiling blue and put clouds on it. As a kid, I thought nothing of it and loved having sleepovers there and imagining flying to each cloud. But now as a landlord, I look at painting differently.

I also include that the landlord has the right to enter the unit with twenty-four hours' written notice to inspect the property from time to time. I don't actually inspect, but the permission is in writing, just in case. I don't need to see how they're living, but some landlords go in every year or so to make sure they haven't taken down the smoke detector and to make sure they've changed the furnace filters, there's no damage to the unit, growth of illegal substances, or so forth.

Should I consider doing leases for shorter than one year?

Sometimes people will be building a new home, so they sell their current home as they need their funds for the construction of the next house. They'll ask for shorter terms, and if it's eight or so months, I will do it. New builds are often behind, so the tenants usually stay longer than initially planned. However, if they've sold one house and are moving to another, and the closing dates are one, two, or three months apart, I don't rent to them. It's too short of a window and not worth the headache for me. Those three months will fly by, and I'll be right back there trying to find a renter again.

Should I have legal counsel look over my lease before I use it with a tenant?

I never have. There's usually a governing body of real estate in the state or province that you can Google, and they will have preprinted leases. For example, in Ontario, it's OREA (Ontario Real Estate Association), and they have forms available that you can fill in.

Every place is different, but legally, in Ontario, you're not supposed to require postdated cheques. Also, you can't discriminate because of pets. But if you fear for your life or see damage to the property because of the four-legged friends, then you have grounds for possible eviction. You can't just say "no pets," or "twelve months postdated cheques required"; however, I have seen it done many times.

What should I do if someone doesn't want to sign a lease or requests I change something?

I wouldn't rent to anyone who didn't want to sign a lease. Otherwise, you're just asking for trouble. I know I don't list anything offside in the lease that they should feel uncomfortable with. If they are making a stink about something, then the door is over there because that means they're a nightmare before it's even started. No one has time for that.

Bbyyyeeee!

Is there anything besides a lease that I should ask for?

Besides the lease, they need to fill out an application that will state how old they are, where they work, where they previously worked, how much they make, if they have a vehicle, what debts they have (school, car, child support, cell phone bill), and why they're moving from their current residence. There should also be somewhere to write down their driver's license number and date of birth.

I don't ask for references as I know I'm probably calling their best friend, mother, or someone who's pretending to be their employer. That's my preference, but if you want to go down that road, knock yourself out. I had a lousy tenant, and the next landlord called to ask for a reference. I said they had never missed rent and were lovely, and if I weren't moving into the unit, I'd let them rent as long as they wanted to, which was one big lie. I know that sounds bad, but that is life. I knew if I told her the truth, she wouldn't rent to them, and I'd be stuck with them. So I don't call references.

Since you never know who you're actually calling, I skip that and go right to social media (their Facebook, Instagram, TikTok, etc.) and creep them. Yep, you read right, a true creeper. For example, this one fellow applied to rent an apartment, and in his profile picture on Facebook, he was holding up two massive bags of weed. It's now legal in Canada, but back then, it wasn't, and he absolutely had enough to be in jail for a long time. New renter? Ya—no thank you, especially when I included utilities and who knows what he would have grown on my dime. Next!

It's also good to see their whole credit report. Are they always late? Do they have creditors after them? I had a lovely lady once fresh off bankruptcy apply for one of my units. I took a chance, and she never once missed rent. I even hired her to do some work here and there because I liked her so much. She was there until I sold the building and still lives there today. I've had other people explain their poor credit, and two months later, they were behind on rent, and I was serving them notices. A lot of landlords will also ask for pay stubs and letters from employers to confirm what the prospective tenants wrote on their applications. Be careful to fully examine any supporting materials they submit with their applications, as you'd be surprised by the number of people who Google things like "good credit score." Then they screenshot a fantastic credit report and send it to prospective landlords. Make sure the information on a credit report is 100% actually them. You should see their name on it, date of birth, address, and other relevant details. If there is just a picture of "803" or what have you and no evidence that it's even them, inquire more to make sure you're not getting punked.

What are some common mistakes I can avoid as a landlord?

Do not rent to someone just because you don't want your unit to sit vacant for a month.

If they're a good tenant and check all the boxes, then move forward. But don't just wing it, and think that anyone in there is better than no money at all. Don't do it! I have been stung many times in thinking that I don't want to show the property again, or I will be leaving the next day for a month, so this is the only couple I can show the property to. Leave it empty unless you're certain that the prospective tenant is exactly who you want in there.

Pay attention to where you place certain tenants.

This is a minor point, but it will still result in lots of phone calls and not the ones you want. Do not put someone with kids above a couple or a single person. The downstairs people will always complain about the upstairs people and the noise they make.

Disclose which areas are "common areas."

If there are shared spaces, say, in a laundry room, storage room, or by the furnace or water heater—and there are multiple units—make sure you tell the tenants it's a common area. They can store things there, but be sure to recommend they don't put valuables inside as it is not locked. I've had tenants say, "I put my snowboard and all my winter purses in here, and now they're gone!" Guess you better call your insurance then renter because I said don't put your valuables in there.

No hot tubs.

I would not have a hot tub at one of my properties, and if you do, then make sure that the tenants pay their own utilities. One time, I had a hot tub at a rental, and when I stopped by, I saw that the hot tub's cover was off. I asked, "Oh, are you going in the hot tub?"

My tenant said, "No."

I said, "Oh, well, I thought you were because the cover is off."

He said, "No, we just like the way the steam looks in the winter with the snowy backdrop."

Oh no, we can't keep the hot tub at 104 degrees just because it looks pretty in the winter—my poor bank account! Dollars evaporating into the winter sky.

That being said, I did actually just purchase a hot tub for an Airbnb of mine. There is often an exception to every rule, and this property is one of those: first, the cost per night is insanely high (which will cover the higher utility bills), and secondly, it's a waterfront property and very popular with the city people. I figure the hot tub will give the winter guests something to do, as the property is not near any ski hills nor any other winter pulls. The beauty of the home and property just draws people, so the hot tub is the cherry on top.

Don't store personal items at long-term rental properties.

I wouldn't leave things at the property, such as a snowblower or electric fireplace, unless you're doing a final walkthrough before you give them the last month's rent back. Otherwise, depending on how they liked you as a landlord, those things may or may not be there when they move out.

Always sign a lease.

I know I said this before, but always signing a lease is important. In the past, I didn't require a lease because I figured that I did enough paperwork in the day, and I didn't need to do any more. Then after one month, a tenant would say he was moving out to go live with his girlfriend, and I'd be back to square one looking for a tenant again. Time management-wise, it's just annoying.

Do a yearly lease so that, at the most, you're there once a year, but hopefully they stay for a couple of years at least.

Serve papers when you should.

If you're busy in your life or think they're good for the money they owe, you should still serve papers and tell the tenant that even if you tear up the paperwork, you still have to do it for the landlord's sake. (Remember: they don't know you're the owner.) If you don't have a property management company, then you should act as the property manager and say that the owner's orders are strict. (What I mean by serving papers are serving those proper notices of eviction should they be late on rent or so forth for your state or province.)

If they don't end up paying, at least the paperwork has already been started toward their eviction, not three weeks after they missed rent when the next month is coming up soon. Also, double-check any papers you have to serve a tenant. If there's a spelling mistake, a math mistake, or the wrong postal code, it could void your document in court, then they get to stay, and you have to start the whole process over again.

Make sure everything is in writing.

You don't ever want a dispute to come down to their word against yours. You don't want to hear, "The landlord didn't tell us we couldn't smoke inside," or "We didn't know we couldn't have eight cars, twelve people living here, and eighteen pets." Make sure everything is written, and you and the tenant(s) sign off on everything and any changes to the original lease are initialed.

Kristin Cripps

Not only do you need to document everything with your tenants but also with your repair people and contractors. I have been screwed so many times when people say, "No, that item wasn't included," or "That's not what I said," etc. With contractors, for example, you can even put daily amounts in the contract. For example, you could include that the job must be finished by Dec 1, 2020, and that for every day past Dec 1, 2020, the contractor will pay the owner $350 per day (or whatever figure makes sense to you). Consider the rent you'd be losing if the contractor falls behind schedule. It's only fair.

Always have extra keys for your properties.

One mistake I commonly make—and have made so many times (I don't seem to learn my lesson)—is failing to have extra keys for properties. If tenants lose a key, then you don't need to pay a locksmith since you have a spare key. If you're renting out short-term, make sure the cleaning person has a spare key. You should have multiple spares, actually, as you will often get messages when people are back in Germany or Australia and they realize they have your front door key.

If possible, try to start and end leases during reasonable times for your climate.

If someone says they want to move in on the first of January (mind you, I live somewhere with lots of snow), not many people want to move at that time of year. You could be in slim pickings time as a landlord if those people moved out in a year to the day. There's a higher chance that with fewer applicants, there won't be as many desirable ones. I find that summer

145

move-ins work best where I live, but maybe you live and rent somewhere where it's summer all year round.

Dealing with maintenance pros

Always get two to four quotes when repairing something important such as a roof.

Speaking of repair people and contractors, be sure to shop quotes. You don't want one person saying your roof is good for five years (which I highly doubt they will as they want to get paid this weekend not five years from now, but just in case).

I've seen people wait until the shingles are curling so badly when they finally replace the roof, it costs them twice as much. Now they have to replace all the sheathing underneath because the water got in and rotted the wood.

How do I decide which maintenance professionals to work with?

If I know a client of mine is a plumber or carpenter, I would rather hire them than randomly look online. I also want to help their business grow and hope that in exchange, they will refer people to my business. Win-win!

I generally use a contractor who was referred to me by a friend or someone I trust. Normally, it works out, but there is the odd time where I would never use them again. If that's the case, then I reference that in my phone so I won't forget. (For example, *Mark Awful Hardwood Floor Installer Never Use Him Again*.)

I don't hire maintenance pros based on deals. Sometimes I'll call four plumbers and use who is available, especially if the water is spewing everywhere. Of those four I call, I will have used them all before. But until you've built those relationships, you'll have to rely on them from their past performance and recommendations or online reviews. If I need a professional in a city where I don't have contacts, I will rely on Google. I might glance at reviews or overall star ratings, but I don't have time to read all those reviews to be completely honest.

When you use the same person repeatedly, they're more likely to give you priority treatment. So if you need a job done ASAP, they will bump someone else to take care of you. They're also more likely to hold off on payment if you have a lot on the go and can't pay them right that second. They're also more likely to not rip you off. Plus, if you do any work on your own home, they'll often give you a better deal as a thank-you.

When they get discounts at tile or vanity stores, for example, they might pass the savings onto you. They'll go to bat for you if the city has issues with permits, or a by-law shows up at your door unexpectedly. And they may agree to do miscellaneous jobs not originally set out but are now required (for free).

The negative to using the same maintenance professionals repeatedly is that they can get too comfortable and think that you won't price shop their quote. For example, they might say, "It will cost $15,000 to build your deck," but then you price the same drawings and get lower quotes for $9,000 to $12,500. That's frustrating, and it stings, but sometimes it happens, including at a much bigger price point. Not every contractor will do this, so I can't paint them all with the same brush.

I always like to work with a contractor who does a job under what they have quoted me. Quite often, you will be quoted one price, and then the project goes over budget. So when I'm quoted $100,000, and it comes in at $81,000, naturally, that makes me want to work with them again.

Sometimes you have to watch out for things you wouldn't expect. I've had contractors ask me on a date, which always makes things awkward afterward. I normally think, "Ugh, why did you have to go and ruin the good thing we had here!" Another time, I had a contractor do two of three units in my triplex. He came to the breakfast place—where I was enjoying a lazy day Sunday breakfast with my girlfriend—and started crying in the restaurant.

He told us all these sob stories about money and how if I could pay for the third unit upfront, it would help him out so much. My girlfriend advised me not to do it, but I'd known him for years. I was in his wedding, I was a godparent to one of his two children, and I'd dated him ages before. So I agreed to help and gave him a bank draft that very same day.

Well, I didn't hear from him for the next three years—and I wouldn't have heard from him at all, but we happened to run into each other. He neither finished my third unit nor returned my money. His brother lived in one of my other rentals and decided since I'd had a falling out with his brother, he would just stop paying rent. Lovely—just what I needed. Thanks, guys!

Should I let my tenants contact these pros, or should I always set up any necessary appointments for the property?

I don't have tenants contact them, but I do have them meet at the home/apartment when the repairs are taking place. I know someone who gave the tenant a contractor's phone number, and the pair ended up pretending things were wrong all the time, and the contractor would "fix" them when nothing was wrong. The contractor would write the owner a bill, and when the owner paid, the tenant and contractor would split the money. As there were never any supplies bought or labor done, it was a fake invoice with free money for the pair. Ever since I heard this story, I have been leery of connecting tenants and contractors.

Most importantly, always be checking their work.

Once, I was continuously giving draws toward a project and busy with other things and travels and didn't make it to the job site for months. When I finally went for a visit, I saw nothing had been done and even the supplies I had put there to be installed had been sold off. Always check for yourself, or have someone else check their work and send you photos and videos if you can't make it there yourself.

I've had people lose me as a client for being unknowledgeable about something and lying. I would rather someone say they didn't know or that isn't their area of expertise, but I will definitely find out for you—as opposed to guessing and pretending they know the answer when they're way off.

Should someone who's just getting started in real estate investing try and run a property long distance, or should they stay local to start out?

My rule has always been that I only buy local within a distance I can easily drive to. Now do I drive to them regularly? No, but I could if I needed to do so. Most of my properties are within five minutes to an hour driving distance from my home.

I go to the cottages every year with my nephews, but I'm not actually checking on the units but enjoying them. I visit two properties every two months or so to deliver toilet paper, shampoo, and paper towels because they're rented short-term. I have other short-term rentals where the cleaning crew gets that kind of stuff. Other properties I only visit when tenants move out. The units where the same tenants have lived there for years, I do not visit. The lawn and snow maintenance is set up, and they pay rent so I don't have a need to visit. Could I check smoke alarms and such? For sure.

I think it's harder and definitely requires more trust of whoever you hire to help you with cleaning, maintenance, and other needs when you add plane rides between you and your properties. If your property will be located farther away from your home, I would use a larger company as opposed to an individual, even if it costs more per month to make sure they're legit and reputable.

If I decide to run a short-term property long distance, what's the first thing I should do?

First, determine who your cleaners are going to be. Are they willing to do other things? For example, if light bulbs or toilet paper are out, will they pick up more? Who will take care of the lawn? Who will purchase new sheets if they get stained or wrecked? With everything online, it isn't hard to do things when you're on a different continent.

Even if you don't have someone responding to guests and you are, you can do it anywhere in the world, and it doesn't take much time at all. The initial set up would be hard to start from out of the area, for short-term rentals, but if this is your scenario, perhaps you could find a company that would furnish it for a certain amount. Buying all the linens, cutlery, accessories, and bedding would be difficult, but maybe it was set up before with a similar rental idea in mind by a previous owner.

I showed a home the other day, and in inclusions where it normally says "fridge," "stove," "window coverings," it listed all those things plus all furniture except personal belongings, and all kitchenware was included. Obviously, they were using it as a cottage or ski chalet and didn't need the stuff; this would be easy and ideal for someone taking over this operation, especially if from afar.

Should I use a local property management service, hire an individual to be a local manager, or do all the work myself?

If afar, you can't do it yourself, so that makes no sense. I have a friend who had trouble with a cleaning lady, so she drove to the property, cleaned it, and drove back. It's a two-and-a-half-hour drive, then she'd clean for two hours and drive back. She charged $200 for the night. What would she have made if she was at work for those seven hours? Deduct that from the $200, and what is she left with? This amount doesn't take into consideration wear and tear on her car, gas money, and cleaning supplies.

It doesn't make sense to do all the work unless you're strapped for cash, but I recommend that you figure out what you're worth. How much do you make a year? Take what you make divided by twelve months, then four weeks, then one week, then five days, assuming you take weekends off, and how many hours you work in each normal day, and see what you're worth hourly.

If you're worth $130 an hour, then why are you doing something you could pay someone $18 an hour to do? But if you're worth $15 an hour, then go do it and suck it up till you're worth more and able to pay someone else to do it. I would suggest that you manage the property and be the landlord until you can afford not to be. Many people want to jump to the front of the line and have everything contracted out, including the property manager, all small and large fixings, maintenance, and so forth. Depending on how tight your numbers are between what you want to make and the desired return, you may need to be that guy or gal in the beginning —at least until you build up a big enough nest egg and get the experience and knowledge in investing necessary before it makes sense to do all the hiring.

If I hire a property management service, what should I expect? How do I choose a good one?

Regarding fees, some property management companies take 10 percent off the get-go, and some take one month's rent. With short-term rental management, I've seen managers take 20 to 35 percent.

To find a good manager, first look for someone referred to you by one or multiple friends. Check their reviews, see that they are a team of professionals. Make sure everything is in writing so they know your expectations and what they do and do not consider part of their job.

I would also get in writing if things are missed. For example, when they miss serving a notice for late rent, they owe you $150; otherwise, they could just shrug it off and say, "Sorry, we weren't able to get there," or "Sorry, we forgot to meet the plumber, and he charged you for that emergency call when it wasn't needed." I had cleaners for one particular property who were supposed to take the garbage out every week regardless of whether it fell on their cleaning day, and unbeknownst to me, they were not doing it. A guest who checked in and had paid $6200+ for the month said it smelt like death and called Airbnb and cancelled. I happened to be close to the property and went over to find what looked like five months of garbage and maggots in the basement. I did not have it in writing what the consequences would be if they missed what we had agreed upon.

Some questions to ask include these: How many years have they been in business? How many staff are in their firm? How many homes/buildings do they look after? Can you have access to references and their current clients?

Google their name, check out their reviews, and see if you can find out which buildings they're looking after. If you find an address, drive by and see how it's maintained. Is there garbage outside? Is the siding falling off? Does it look like the building has been through a hurricane, but there hasn't been a hurricane for over thirty years? Or does the building look pristine with quality tenants around?

If I do all the work myself, how often should I be in contact with my tenants? How often should I visit the property?

I have my tenants set up to pay online. I know clients who drive around because they like to pick up cash, which is too time-consuming to me; I like the ease of pushing "accept." I only visit when they tell me they're moving, but that's probably not what you should do until you have some time and experience under your belt. You should visit your properties when you can and make sure nothing is damaged inside. Perhaps bring them a new furnace filter, and check that the smoke detector and carbon monoxide detectors are working. If you don't want to meet with your tenants regularly, then drive by periodically to eyeball the property.

Be sure you can trust who you hire. I had someone tell a client of mine that they couldn't rent his property. He wasn't sure why it wasn't renting, so he secret-shopped the manager and was told there was a glitch online and that the property was not available when it actually was. The owner drove up to find that the property manager was having a big cottage party with all his friends in the owner's rental!

Part 6

Masterclass

In my experience, in the real-estate business past success stories are generally not applicable to new situations. We must continually reinvent ourselves, responding to changing times with innovative new business models.

—Akira Mori, real estate developer

Stupid mistakes (and how to avoid them)

Do you know that saying about how experience is the best teacher? Well, like most sayings, it's true. However, I'd like to offer some advice that could save you the trouble most folks have to learn the hard way. Pay close attention here, and you'll save yourself a lot of time, trouble, and heartache.

What are some dos and don'ts when starting out with investment properties?

Don't buy a house just because it's a power of sale or in foreclosure

Do your homework.

(Yes, I'm saying it again!)

Is the home actually priced below market value? If so, then it's fine to purchase if you're looking for a deal as long as it doesn't mess up your financing. Many people assume these types of properties are naturally good deals, but often that's not the case. Many people also assume that if they are approved for $500,000, then they can buy a $400,000 power of sale. However, banks like homes in good or better-than-good condition, so even if the asking price is below what you were approved for, they could deny your financing.

Don't guesstimate costs for renovations when you haven't done proper research to discover what something really costs.

Don't assume it will be $3,000 for the floors, $5,000 for the kitchen, and $15,000 to finish the basement, then add three large windows. You could easily find out that your floors are $12,000, not counting installation; kitchen counters are $7,000, not counting appliances, cupboards, backsplash, lighting or hardware; and $40,000 for the basement, not counting the addition of the new windows. Know the full and accurate financial picture before you pull the trigger.

Don't listen to people who have no experience in investing.

Do your research. I feel like that's what I have written for the past three answers ('cuz it is). Read books on the topic, listen to podcasts, or maybe take some online courses. Why would you take investment advice from your sister who still lives with Mom and Dad?

Don't think that just because you've spent $40,000 on renovations, you will automatically get $40,000 or more out of that project.

I've seen this, heard it, and had it pointed out to me in person—and I am always rolling my eyes. Someone will say, "Well, we had this custom banquette made from blah blah wood shipped from blah blah for X amount of money, and we know we will get it all back when we sell."

Nope. Not everyone wants that, and those who do are probably not going to spend the $8,000 you spent to have it made. They might—I repeat *might*—give you $500 to $1,500 at most.

I had a lady who said her rain head shower cost $4,200 as it was made by a certain designer. Well, good for that designer for getting that much money from you because you can buy one on Wayfair for less than $399, and probably under $200, if you really look, and 99.9 percent of people won't know the difference between the two. Just because you spend that amount of money doesn't mean it will be returned to your pocket. (Sorry if this upsets you, but I'm going to tell you the facts, not just what you want to hear.)

Don't think that if you put $30,000 into *any* house that you can sell it for $100,000 more.

I know you've probably watched all the renovation and flipping shows that often show massive profit and gain, and I watch them too, so you're not alone. However, behind the scenes, these people have already done all their homework and are searching for a needle in the haystack.

They're not picking just any haystack and dumping money into it and expecting a money tree to magically grow and replenish their bank accounts. They're precisely dissecting their costs and profit while knowing the markets and neighbourhoods and where they can save money.

I'm not sure why someone would think that just because they watched thirty minutes of a program where someone bought a home for $250,000, spent $30,000 putting in a new kitchen, ensuite, and painted the outside, listed it for $389,000, then sold it for $380,000, that it's possible with just any property.

It's not.

Don't get me wrong; I'm not the glass-is-half-empty girl, but I am the *realistic* girl looking at the glass, the type of glass, the size of the glass, whether the water is bottled, tap, or filtered. I ask whether there is a jug around and what the other glasses look like. You need to look at the whole picture so you can feel confident that you're investing your money properly to get that massive gain.

Don't think you can buy a property with someone else to save on cost and naively think you will both equally work on and invest the time into the property.

I've also seen a lot of "friends" buy together, and they're not usually friends the next time I see one of them. If you do decide to buy with a friend, make sure a lawyer does the paperwork for you and details everything!

Are you putting more money in than they are?

Are you supposed to split the utilities or the planned renovations 50/50?

If you're buying a cottage, do you both get to use it for one month in the summer with your family?

Is one person paying for the supplies and the other doing the work?

Even if you think part of your agreement includes minuscule points, document them. I've seen people fight over just about everything. Plan everything, and have it all scheduled on paper and signed by both parties. Show that both parties have had the right to review and seek their own legal counsel for the agreement.

Even if it's not a friendship or platonic venture, I have also seen a boyfriend and girlfriend or spouses argue about a project, when one person doesn't keep up with their share of the obligations—be that lawn maintenance or cleaning of the house. Someone starts to party more than the other, and there are unwanted guests at the residence. One person wants to put in new light fixtures, and the other thinks there's nothing wrong with the ones they have. Someone wants to widen the driveway while the other doesn't. Someone says we need a new roof; the other says the one they have still had five years left. And when it's done, the one wants to replace it with asphalt shingles and the other wants to have a steel roof installed. Someone wants to put up a fence or add a pool, and the other doesn't want to spend the money.

If you're buying or flipping a property with a family member, friend, partner, or strictly for business, it's still a relationship where you need to mesh well together. If it's just bickering and fighting over the house and money, then what fun is that? Make sure everything is in black and white, so both parties know beforehand what is expected of them, their bank accounts, their time frames, and so forth.

Don't have unrealistic timelines for work to be done without giving yourself "hiccup" room.

I wish I could say that everything is on schedule and has always been for every project I've ever done, but I can't think of one that finished when it was supposed to. Whether I'm behind in getting the "pretty" things to my contractors, have a sick contractor, a delay in permits from the city, a discontinued item that means four more weeks to get something else, a wrong counter or vanity or flooring showing up, or we find surprises behind walls—be those electrical issues, old plumbing, termites, or rodents—there's *always* some form of a hiccup.

Leave yourself extra time and build that into your budget for holding the mortgage, your move-in date, or whatever that looks like for your project. If you have ever bought a new build in a subdivision, you know it's the same. Even though they've probably built tens of thousands of homes and subdivisions—and you would think they'd have it down like clockwork—they're often months and even sometimes years behind target and schedule.

Don't look only at the best-case scenarios without considering the worst case when running numbers.

A severe rookie mistake is only looking at the lowest price to do your renovations without considering what could happen. Look at the cost of the roof, the flooring, the kitchen, the bathrooms, and the windows. You could surprisingly find out that you need to do your eaves troughs or gutters or that the vanity you wanted is out of stock, and now you're paying $1,000 more. To think that you are not going to have any added costs at all is naive. You might not be able to save your attic insulation, and it could all need to be redone. Or the flooring you thought you could sand and recoat/stain but turns out not to be salvageable.

I advise you to add in extras and uh-ohs, so you're not surprised with an unexpected bill at the end. Make sure the potentially higher renovation costs still make sense to you and your endgame. If they do, then you know you've found a property to live in, buy as an investment, or flip.

Don't think you're going to snap your fingers without realizing you're going to need to do work.

You know those fun or inspirational sayings you see on photos and wall art? I have so many of those in my homes and staging warehouse, but that doesn't mean I think life and investing are all one-liners or catchy phrases and easy breezy. Believe me, I know there's hard work involved to reach that peak and summit. That optimal life takes energy and consciousness, learning and constantly reinventing to stay there, and, of course, action.

There are phrases about imagining it, dreaming it, and achieving it, and then there's action. There's a saying that goes, "Don't talk, act. Don't say, show. Don't promise, prove." There are going to be either physical things you'll need to do in the job, or systems you need in place for other people, contractors, and assistants to run it smoothly. Once you've done the sleepless nights and put in the legwork, then it's more a snap of the fingers or a flip of the switch. But don't think it's like that right from the beginning. It takes time, practice, knowledge, learning, experimentation, and research to build your real estate empire.

Don't think everything is as easy as you see on TV shows.

I like that not all the renovation shows indicate that a profit has been made; however, almost 100 percent of them show a profit. Why do they primarily show people making tons of money in small time frames when that would not always be the case? I would like to know the whole picture and be educated before I spend tens or hundreds of thousands of dollars. That just seems logical to me when so much is on the line.

I've seen programs where the host said, "If I sell it right now, I break even, and every week after that, I lose money." Some show a grand loss of $20,000 to $50,000 or more. I think this is good because unlike an infomercial for a stationary bicycle, stair climber, or diet pill, people are often putting every penny they have in a real estate deal, and it's much more costly than some of these examples.

The stakes are high, and it's not something one should take lightly. Know there are risks and I know I keep harping, but research the sold properties, the current competition, the trends in the neighbourhoods, and what is planned for the town or city, and know what the growth is like. Don't go blind into any investment. I'm not trying to be a Debbie Downer, and there is money to be made in real estate, but you can also lose money in real estate. Make sure you have a grasp on the whole picture before you dive into the pool.

Look at *all* the costs of flipping.

Don't only see the purchase price and renovation cost while forgetting about holding it for X months, real estate fees, transfer taxes, capital gains, staging, higher insurance since it's sitting vacant, etc. Many people see black and white but forget about all the other shades in the spectrum. Make sure when you're doing your calculations and spreadsheets when contemplating offering on a property, or when in your conditional period, that you're not missing any costs.

Don't forget lawyer fees, the cost to discharge the mortgage and for staging per month. I understand the excitement and enthusiasm for real estate, and I think it's fantastic, but I don't want you to be disappointed. If you forget about the other things you have to pay for, you won't make as much profit in the end and could potentially go in the negative.

You'll have utility bills while you hold the property and set up fees for those utilities. Maybe there's only propane to the property, and you want natural gas to demand more from the market when selling, and that has a large price for the initial hookup. Okay, that's not necessarily true. It depends if gas is at the road, and if it's not, how far it is would determine your cost. Don't forget all your real estate fees, transfer fees, and taxes. How much does the state, province, country where you live want for their piece of the pie for what you made? Normally, insurance companies jack their insurance when it's vacant because the risk of it being broken into skyrockets, so have you included this in your budgeting? I apologize if you think this is overwhelming; I am just trying to make you informed.

Don't forget if you're going to rent that you will have vacant months.

Say, the unit is ready August 1, but no one can move in until October 1. Have you budgeted for this lull? When I have tenants tell me they are moving out on X date, I show their unit one to three times before they move out so I can line up the current tenants moving out and the new tenants moving in for the same day. That way, I don't have that "cricket" empty bank account time.

If you're buying a turnkey home, and there's nothing to do, then you can use your walkthroughs to line up tenants for the day you get possession. Then you will have no time where no one's paying you—whether short or long-term rental, you're not left holding the bag and can start collecting the money the day you get possession. I purchased a cottage in a place of three towns known as "cottage country" and asked the current owners if I could advertise it before I took possession on a short-term rental site, and they agreed.

They were leaving all their furniture and dishes and rafts, so the only change was whose name was going to be on the deed. I had it rented from the tenth of August (my possession date) until the thirtieth of November when I took it off the site so I could start renovations before I had a key or even owned the property. Naturally, the only time you can't do this is when you're buying the property and renovating; otherwise, you can start to advertise as soon as you've firmed up on the property. I recommend first getting the current owner's permission in writing since you don't officially own it yet. If you're renovating, you could still advertise it and tell prospective renters that these floors will be in or this will be the bathroom with this vanity and try to make the time from your possession to finish renovations as short as possible.

Don't forget to add appliances to your pricing.

A lot of people will screenshot a kitchen from IKEA or some built-in home hardware centre, but it won't include their appliances. Appliances can quickly tack on $2,000, $3,000, or even over $10,000, depending on the brand you're buying. Make sure you know if you need to change a washing machine and dryer or if the wine fridge works. Calculate everything so there are no extra surprises for you (besides the ones behind the walls that you have already guesstimated).

Don't think if you're going to do it yourself, that it will show well.

At one of my properties, I didn't let my laminate sit in the home and acclimatize first before having it installed. Fast-forward a year, and it was gappy and looked horrible, and it had swollen (or "unswollen," I'm not sure what it really does). It looked like junk.

I went to the store where I bought it, and the employee said I should have allowed the laminate to acclimatize and adjust to the room temperature for two to three days before it was installed. While that was great advice, it would have been nice to know that before I installed it, though. She said, "Everyone knows that." Well, I didn't, but I do now and won't forget.

I also made the mistake of doing my first basement myself. I thought I would take every Saturday off from massaging and instead work on my house then bartend at night. I was not so great with making walls the straightest or blending the mud after dry-walling, cutting the edges of the carpet, and doing that whole kick thing with your knee to get the carpet tight. I should have paid someone to do it as opposed to a having choppy-ass basement.

I also shouldn't paint myself. At one property, I put all the green painters edging tape around. Painted the five coats (yes, five coats as it was a red room—styles change, don't judge me), and spread out over months as I didn't have a lot of time. When I finally peeled the green off, it took some red with it and showed some of the grey primer. I ended up putting crown molding over it because it was too messy to attempt to fix.

Don't over-renovate your property; consider the whole picture and who your neighbours are.

When you run your numbers for renovating the kitchen, bathrooms, and roof, for example, take the property into account. Pay attention, especially if it backs onto a wrecking yard, has a gas station two houses away, and the neighbour has eight cars on their front lawn, not counting what's in the driveway. Just because homes have sold in the neighbourhood at the price you want doesn't mean they have the same neighbouring hindrances.

Don't spend too much on renovations.

For example, don't buy flooring that looks a smidge different than another flooring but is double the price and then expect to get that price back out. If you're flipping the property, and there are two white shaker cupboards you can buy—one for the whole kitchen is $5,000, and another better quality for the same style is $25,000—buy the cheaper one.

If you can purchase trim for your entire house for $1,200 instead of $6,000, go with the cheaper one. Is it pine, is it MDF? Are you going to live in this house and want a certain type, or is it a flip or rental? Make sure you weigh everything into your decisions. I've seen vanities that all look identical with the slightest of variances, one may be $800, one $1,900, one $5,475, and one $12,600. Really consider if this is something where you can recoup your money. Now I don't knock you if you know you won't get the money out or don't care, and it's your dream house. That's totally fine, but if that's not the case, then do your homework and don't overpay.

Don't get too attached to a house.

The more attached to the house you are, the higher the chance you will pay more than you need to in negotiations. There will always be other homes/investments! Try to keep your feelings and enthusiasm separate. Go onto the next one if they won't sell to you for the price you're willing to pay.

Also, a lot of people get "stars in their eyes" when they see the kitchen or the walk-in closet as big as their current master bedroom. Then they get blinders to the rest of the house, neighbourhood, or price point. They don't care that it's priced $150,000 over the market, that the neighbourhood is crap, or that it backs onto a car-crushing plant. Look at the home objectively and subjectively—not just emotionally and visually.

This next story is more sad than stupid, and I feel bad for the woman to whom it happened. I sold her home in the city where I live, and she was driving around the country one day and saw a private "for sale by owner" sign at an open house and wandered in. The land was acreage and serene and had a bungalow on it, which was perfect for her arthritic knees.

She privately purchased the property with no home inspection and no realtor on either side. After closing on the home, she saw that the house did not only have knob-and-tube wiring but also asbestos. But worse than that, the property had been a landfill in the '60s and '70s, and there were massive environmental cleanup bills never disclosed to her.

The seller had lied and pretended it was "as is" because his mother lived there, and he didn't know much about the house, but it was because he didn't want to tell her about the landfill.

Fast-forward four years later, and she is still in court fighting him, and I pray that it's sorted in her favour sooner rather than later as this is not how she planned to spend her retirement right after her husband of decades passed. The moral of this story is to have a realtor protecting your interest, who will also have insurance to protect you even if they aren't knowledgeable enough themselves. If you don't have a realtor, then make sure you have a great lawyer, who is very thorough and not rushing through the process.

Don't buy a home just because the street name is the same as your name.

If you think, "Well, the house isn't too bad, and it would be so cool to live on *my* street," well, this is super stupid and amateur. Buy a house for the house, the neighbourhood, what you love about it such as the backyard or kitchen, but not the street name. You may wonder, "Why does she even have to say that?" but I've seen it done at least thirty times during my career, if not more, so that's why I have to say it.

Don't buy the house the "first" day it's on the market and think you scooped it up before anyone else.

That may be absolutely true, however, for a family member of mine who will remain nameless (I apologize if you read this and know it's you) who said, "It had only been listed a few hours, so we had to move fast, and that's why we gave them the full asking price."

Well, I pulled up the listing, and while it was listed that day, it was also listed for four consecutive months before that with no offers, and they cancelled and relisted it, and bait, line, and sinker, they got what they wanted. Make sure your realtor or someone in your corner checks out the history of the property so you know how many days it has actually been on the market and know the comparable sales and true value of the home/condo/apartment complex.

Don't buy something not on a sturdy, solid foundation unless you have the funds to fix it.

I think it's silly when people buy an old cottage and think they can just put a massive addition on it and cash in, but they don't look at the foundation. Often, there isn't a foundation at all, and the house is on piers. I've seen cinder blocks and posts on forty-five-degree angles.

On one occasion, the home inspector grabbed me and the buyer and asked us to come look at something. He looked at our feet and saw we were wearing flip-flops and asked, "Do you own running shoes?"

I thought it was odd, but answered, "Yes."

He said, "Then run far away from this house." He proceeded inside and started to push the insulation out of the house from the inside, then poked his hand through. It was crazy; I had never seen something like that and haven't seen it since.

My buyer still bought the house! Even though she did get a substantial discount, he said it didn't matter if they gave her $80,000 off—he still suggested she didn't buy it.

Don't buy without doing the research or reviewing the research your realtor sends your way.

I had a client say he wanted to offer $600,000 for a home listed for $609,000. I'm sure you're thinking that that seems reasonable; however, all the comparables in the area and similar were selling in the $520,000–$535,000 max range. He said, "You can send them to me if you have to, but I'm not going to look at them."

I thought that was not the brightest decision, but he wanted the house, and so be it. I think it's easier to see mistakes in other people's decisions more so than our own. Call them our blind spots; call it what you like. However, at least he knew the comparables were $520,000 and $535,000 before and didn't find out after he took possession of his new home. That wouldn't have been a fun realization.

Don't get into a place that's over your head.

Let's say that you're approved for $400,000 but know that your wife is going to stop working soon as you're going to start a family. Or maybe you're hoping to go back to school. You'll be crying a river when you can't afford your payments. You knew before you bought it, so why did you buy such an expensive house? Some job losses and pregnancies are not planned, but when they are, some people still buy homes in a higher price bracket than they rationally should.

Don't buy a place without parking.

Unless you live somewhere where it's common, like a major metropolitan city where everyone takes the subway or tube, make sure you have parking. For example, in the city where I live, there was a duplex for sale where you had to drive over two other people's properties to get to the parking. If they had cars parked on those other two properties, your tenants wouldn't be able to get to the parking at your unit, nor would they be able to leave in the morning for work if they were blocked in. So the type of tenants they were attracting, being that it wasn't on a bus route and not close enough to walk to anything, was less than ideal and proved to be an extreme stumbling block in selling that property now and I'm sure would be the same in the future.

Part 7

What's Next?

The best investment on Earth is earth.
                                    —Louis Glickman, real estate investor

How do you decide on your long-term investment plan? It depends on how big your goal is. Do you want extra money every month to cover your kids' extracurricular activities, or do you want to go from full-time to part-time work or quit completely and be a millionaire? What you want determines how much you will need to expand.

Expanding your empire/long-term investment plans

Most people find that running real estate investment rentals is either for them or not. Having two and fifteen are not much different, so if you are good with having rentals and don't stress if something needs to be repaired or a tenant breaks the lease, or there's a raccoon in the attic, why not buy more and grow your empire and wealth? If the first sign of something sideways sends you into a panic zone, then the real estate investment business isn't for you and you definitely shouldn't buy more.

What's your advice to someone who wants to expand their empire?

Don't pretend you're some big investor when you're not. Go at a pace that the bank will lend to you, and only do private loans if they're short-term, when you have a lot of buffer, and it still makes financial sense. Some people see twenty deals and want to buy all twenty but can only afford to do three. Don't stretch yourself too thin!

There may come a time when you can easily afford twenty properties, but until you have the money in the bank and an extra cushion, perhaps now is not that time. Take your time, and win the race properly. Don't fall flat on your face and realize that you're drowning in renovations, contractor costs, and other fees when you didn't have to.

Some people get too big too fast. I recommend that you take bite-sized portions; do not stuff your face and choke to death. I know you see the dollar signs, and you want to fast-forward to the endgame, but like they say, Rome wasn't built in a day. Were the Romans working toward building Rome? Of course, but they didn't just snap their fingers, and—voilà—there was Rome. They mindfully built brick by brick, stone by stone, and with a planned, bigger vision in mind—and it still took a thousand years to build Rome!

Don't get in over your head. I know you're tough, and you believe you can handle it (and I don't doubt that you can), but take steps, and you don't need to call them baby steps if that offends you. You don't need to be running and jumping over those high hurdles right from the get-go. Wait until you've walked the track and know where the pavement is uneven, where that weed sticks out, where your shoelace always seems to come untied, and know where your hamstring likes to give out.

What do I do if the bank won't lend to me anymore?

In Canada, there are certain banks that lend up to six properties and others that lend up to ten units, then after ten, it's much more difficult. You have to decide if it's worth it. Some may say that if you have over ten properties, then you shouldn't need a bank. I have exercised this option in the past. I didn't want to buy it outright, but the bank wouldn't finance me, so I sucked it up and said, "Fine, I will buy it myself," stuck out my tongue at them in my head like a four-year-old, and purchased it with no mortgage—cash.

I bought a power of sale, and the bank said, "They wanted it well-maintained and in good condition." Obviously, this property was neither of the two, so they said no. I got a private mortgage, did the renovations, and reapproached the bank. They sent an appraiser out and then agreed to finance it. I went from a 10-percent interest-only loan with a private individual to 2.39 percent with a bank five months later.

Also, maybe they won't lend to you because you haven't done your taxes in a few years. If you get that done, then perhaps you can get out of any "loan shark" type loan and into something that makes more financial sense.

I would see if the numbers make sense at a private. What if you had to stay with the private lender? If you can't get the money, and you don't have the money, then I'd say it's a slippery slope, and I would take it as a sign that it's not the right time. Perhaps you need to clean up your credit, get your taxes done, or stay at the job longer so you have another income tax return showing your job stability or so forth.

How should my investment strategy change as my portfolio grows?

In my case, I want more return. What I used to get out of bed for, I won't anymore. I imagine that it's pretty universal across the board around the evolution of investing. You think $100 is a lot of money when you're a kid, and then you get older, and $1000 is a lot of money. With a few thousand dollars, you could buy a beater car when you're sixteen years old.

Then it goes to $10,000 as you start to think about schooling and education and student loans and how long it will take you to pay off however many years you go to school. Then you start to think of hundreds of thousands and buying a home, and as you start investing, maybe your goal is ten houses or a million dollars. But as you reach that pinnacle, you realize a million won't get you very far, and you already have the knack for investing, so why not make it three, five, ten or twenty million?

That's the story of evolution and growing your wealth. I started loving multifamily units. Then I switched to preferring short-term rentals, whether those be cottages on water or in city centers for visiting tourists. I also went from buying old houses aged fifty to one hundred years to doing new construction. It's not that I wouldn't have loved new builds originally, but they were not in my budget, and I couldn't make them happen. I needed to make my money in older homes to increase my options in the future.

Kristin Cripps

Back in the day, I would have done a flip for $35,000. However, a couple of weeks ago, someone offered me eight figures for a project of mine, and I said I wasn't selling. I would rather keep that investment for my design desires and future revenue. That money was not enough to excite me, whereas back in the day, if someone had offered me $200,000, I think I'd pee my pants with excitement and think I won the lottery!

Conclusion

I am passionate about helping others live their best lives. That's why I find it heartbreaking when people say they live vicariously through other people. What one would do with unlimited wealth versus what another would do is totally different. Why watch what other people do, only to say, "I wish she had given to a particular charity or started a foundation or travelled to a specific country."

Instead, why not rock your greatness and create your life and paint your own dreams?

With social media we could disappear for hours and get lost in videos, memes, gifs, stories, and feeds—but how long will you wait until you start creating your reel?

Some say they're too young, don't have the schooling, the knowledge, the funds, or the time. Others say they're too old, no one will listen to them, it's too late, they missed the boat, and maybe it will happen for them in the next life (if there is a next life).

There will never be a more perfect time than right now! So get out of your excuses, decide what you want, desire, and dream about, start taking the steps that you celebrate along the way, and go after it!

Naturally, I believe that real estate investing can help you live your best life. Depending on your job or profession, real estate investing can make money for you faster than most traditional setups. The number of times I've heard clients say, "We'll just stay renting, save longer, and buy later" is beyond countable or comprehensible.

For example, I met a young couple at an open house who had been approved for a $300,000 mortgage counting their down payment. They offered on a property with me listed for $319,000. They were accepted at $310,000 as the bank approved the slight extra, and they had to pay off a credit card. But after the home inspection, there was around $5,000 of issues, fixes, and concerns that came up. We requested that the items be fixed or the repair money be discounted from the sellers, but we were refused. The young couple decided to walk from the deal to continue renting and saving more money.

Fast-forward six years later, and that house with no neighbours behind, with a good-sized lot, and on a desirable cul-de-sac was selling in the $670,000 to $700,000 range. By then, the couple had two children and daycare costs, but had moved up in their jobs and had better credit. While they could secure an A lender instead of a B lender, they were approved for $380,000 but couldn't afford to get into the market as the homes in that price point were condominiums, had common element fees, which puts them over the $380,000, and they didn't like the neighbourhoods. They were forced to move four hours north for cheaper housing and had to take a pay cut in their jobs to try and save up there.

If they had just gotten in the market and let the house go up in value and save for them, they could have had a substantial nest egg by now. Perhaps they could have pulled out that extra money and bought a few rental properties, which would have also made them money every month and gone up in value and paid those mortgages down a bit.

Having that extra money earned in real estate investing allows you to do things that living pay cheque to pay cheque doesn't allow you to do.

How many of these items are on your "maybe" list:

☐ Maybe you want to go on more vacations.

☐ Maybe you want a car for your parents or your sibling.

☐ Maybe you want to put your child in competitive cheerleading or lacrosse or hockey.

☐ Maybe you want to put your aunt in a better nursing home.

☐ Maybe you want to invest in a startup company you really believe in.

☐ Maybe you want to give to a charity.

☐ Maybe you want to renovate your home or move altogether.

☐ Maybe you want to get some special therapy for your child.

☐ Maybe your friend needs medical treatment that is not covered by their insurance, and you'd like to help out.

Real estate wealth gives you the freedom to do other things that having a "job" doesn't necessarily allow you to. How do you figure out what your best life looks like? You can start by envisioning, journaling, and making lists.

What do you see?

What do you want?

What would you like to have in your life?

Do you want a walk-in closet the size of your current living room? Maybe what you want is not material at all; maybe you want to help children receive better schooling or have food on their tables or access to clean drinking water. Maybe you want to invent something.

The more downtime you give yourself to journal, visualize, meditate, and be away from technology and screens, the better able you can see what's underneath all the everyday traffic, drama, and chaos on the surface. You may have never thought of doing something, but then you run across someone who suddenly sparks a light bulb idea that sends you on a completely different trajectory.

I encourage you to be accepting of the changing path. I took a course ten months ago where we journaled and divided our lives into twelve parts and wrote what we wanted in those areas. If I were to write one now, it would be probably 40 percent the same and 60 percent new. This doesn't mean I'm spinning my wheels and going nowhere; it means I'm getting more fine-tuned and precise about what I want and how I'm going to get to that outcome.

You should listen to affirmations, say affirmations, sit quietly, and whether that be with your eyes closed and calm music, a journal and pen in your hand, a paintbrush and blank canvas, or sweating like a maniac on a stationary bike at the gym, just clear your mind, and see what comes to the surface. Take note of what comes up. Is it positive or negative? Is it a past belief? Is there any truth to it? Is it serving you or standing in your way?

It's important to see what's working in your life and what isn't. Examine any negative thoughts you have about yourself. What future outcomes are you afraid may happen? What happens if they don't happen, and you never tried because of those fears? What would you regret? What could you miss out on? How could what you missed out on spiraled and webbed into something so much bigger and grander and expansive to you and those you love?

When you're successful with real estate investing, copy and repeat. Do what you love and what lights you up. Spend time with your loved ones. Do the things you don't need to make money at doing, but you do it because you want to, and it brings you true joy.

Encourage and help others to go after their dreams. Living out your dreams can be lonely, so it's good to have a tribe, village, city, or world beside you conquering their dreams as well. Then you can all share, encourage, give ideas, give support, give recommendations of things to avoid, and pitfalls to watch out for.

Live life with the most umph you can. Look at life through the eyes of a child, filled with imagination and possibility. Remove anything that has happened, which holds you in the past or fear, and live in today and create your tomorrow.

I am doing what I want to do because my heart is drawn to it, regardless of how it affects my bank account. I enjoy showing others how to live better lives, love themselves, forgive themselves, forgive others, have healthy routines, and break through any "barrier" on their highway to success.

As I said, I believe everyone should be living their best life; everyone deserves their best life and to be the best version of themselves.

For me, this looks like speaking wherever I can, including podcasts, interviews, shows, seminars, summits, and talks. I'm going to be vulnerable, real, and the best me I can be. I am going to better myself for me and those with whom I cross paths. I am going to start a home decor, home renovation, and clothing line. I'm going to continue writing books, doing docuseries, making online courses and content. I'm going to continue travelling, exploring, taking time for myself and loved ones, smiling, laughing, playing, not fearing judgement, and just being me.

I look forward to seeing you along the journey, accomplishing all of your dreams, playing full out and letting nothing stand in your way. You deserve this, you've got this, and you will succeed! Much love.

Acknowledgements

Thank you for taking the time to read this. Thank you for wanting to live a better version of your life and knowing that real estate can be that for you. I am so excited for you and your journey! Do not be a stranger, we are all in this together.

Much love to you and all those you care for.

About the Author

Kristin Cripps is a prolific real estate investor and developer who's crushing it in the world of business. Although she left home at age sixteen, she was able to purchase her first property at age nineteen—becoming a millionaire before the age of thirty.

A former bartender, waitress, and massage therapist turned real estate mogul, today, Kristin is a highly sought-after international wealth creation coach, speaker, and trainer, who consistently features in the top 1 percent of property brokers in Canada.

Kristin is on a mission to show others how to acquire financial freedom and live a life of abundance and contentment through her proven real estate investment strategies and mindset reset techniques.

This unstoppable woman travels the world to share the *anyone-can-do-it* strategies she used to create massive success. She can often be found abroad, searching for inspiration in unique architectural design while fulfilling her quest for constant learning, growth, and development.

Despite the remarkable wealth she's created from a standing start, she is incredibly grounded and loves spending time with her family and amazing circle of loyal friends, colleagues, and her award-winning team at Cripps Realty.

CPSIA information can be obtained
at www.ICGtesting.com
Printed in the USA
BVHW071726231220
596247BV00001B/4